BEING SMART IS STUPID

BEING SMART IS STUPID

Why Embracing the Wisdom of Your Buddha
Nature is the Secret to Great Leadership

TRICIA BROUK

THE BIG TALK *press*

Visit the author's websites at:
https://triciabrouk.com/

Published and distributed by Big Talk Press
New York, USA
www.thebigtalkpress.com

Library of Congress Control Number: 2025911791
Brouk, Tricia
Being Smart Is Stupid: Why Embracing the Wisdom of Your Buddha Nature is the Secret to Great Leadership

ISBN:
Paperback 978-1-960553-07-2
Hardcover 978-1-960553-05-8
eBook 978-1-960553-06-5

To Joe . . . thank you for being curious about Buddha nature and living alongside mine.

And to Lola and Bella . . . thank you for teaching me the tenderness of impermanence in real time.

ALSO BY TRICIA BROUK

The Influential Voice
Saying What You Mean For
Lasting Legacy

The Invitation
Vital Conversations
About Menopause

What people are saying about
BEING SMART IS STUPID

Tricia Brouk has done it again. In *Being Smart is Stupid*, she masterfully dismantles the myth that raw intellect and relentless hustle are the keys to leadership success. This book is a revelation. Tricia's storytelling, drawn from her own remarkable journey and the lives of those she's impacted, is as inspiring as it is practical. She doesn't just tell us to lead with wisdom; she shows us how to cultivate stillness, gratitude, and compassion in ways that transform not only our leadership, but also our lives. For anyone who's ever felt the weight of leadership or questioned the true meaning of success, this book is your guide to leading with authenticity, intention, and impact. Tricia Brouk is a force of nature, and this book is her gift to leaders everywhere.

George Andriopoulos,
CEO of Launchpad Five One Six, Co-Founder of SPEAK

Many leaders are trying to hold onto what worked in the past because it's never been harder to predict the way forward. In *Being Smart Is Stupid: Why Embracing the Wisdom of Your Buddha Nature is the Secret to Great Leadership*, renowned entrepreneur and public speaking coach Tricia Brouk offers a positive and practical alternative: letting go of the need to grasp for control, tapping our inner wisdom and embracing discernment to lead our team to new heights. It's inspiring and essential reading for right now.

Elaine Pofeldt,
independent journalist and author of
The Million-Dollar, One-Person Business

This book is brilliant. Truly brilliant. I could give you a play-by-play run-down of the book, and so what, it would just be one guy's opinion. The gift of this book is a look inside Tricia's soul.

This is a book on leadership, and in the world today, that is a resource greatly lacking. I know Tricia and have experienced her leadership firsthand. This book is a perfect explanation of her power, humanity, and highly effective brand of leadership.

Please read this book, and as she says, reading it is not enough. Take on the practices, use it as a resource and witness how much things change, especially with those around you. With well over 50,000 books on leadership published, this one will stand out, give yourself the gift of its wisdom.

Mike Shereck,
Executive coach, EOS Implementer, author

As someone who has experienced boardrooms, classrooms, speaking stages, online spaces, and places of worship across four continents, I've seen the full spectrum of leadership—from the loud and domineering to the quietly transformational. This book is a beautiful invitation to the latter. It is a reminder that the most resonant leadership doesn't shout; it listens. It doesn't seek control; it seeks understanding. Leading with Buddha nature is not a concept—it's a practice, one that this book gently and powerfully brings to life. For those of us committed to leading with clarity, grace, and global humanity, this is a must read.

Ekpedeme "Pamay" Bassey,
Chief Learning and Diversity Officer
for the Kraft Heinz Company

This book serves as a powerful reminder that the most effective leadership begins not with control, but with stillness and self-awareness. *Being Smart is Stupid: Why Embracing the Wisdom of Your Buddha Nature is the Secret to Great Leadership* challenges conventional models of power and instead offers a deeply human, spiritually grounded approach to leading. It speaks to the leader in all of us—the one who listens before acting and leads by being, not doing. I found these lessons incredibly impactful in work and life. I urge you to tune into Tricia Brouk's leadership wisdom.

Lisa Wheeler,
Emmy-nominated Executive Producer and
two-time *New York Times* Best Selling author

This insightful book beautifully presents practical Buddhist philosophy in accessible guidelines, enriching everyday life with clarity, compassion, and mindfulness. Its timeless wisdom inspires calm, balance, and thoughtful action, making it an invaluable companion for anyone seeking peace and purpose in the modern world. Practical and profound. Guiding and grounded. Handy and honed. Truly enlightening and empowering.

Jerry Farnett,
LCSW, CASAC Master Counselor

Compassion, presence, and inner wisdom are essential elements of the kind of grounded, authentic power that enables us to have lasting impact. By blending timeless Buddhist practices with contemporary leadership insights, Tricia Brouk offers a clear path to influencing others by discovering what is best and truest in ourselves. *Being Smart is Stupid* is as wonderful as its title.

Sally Helgesen,
author, *How Women Rise,*
Rising Together, The Web of Inclusion

This book is a reminder that personal growth isn't just about big breakthroughs but also about paying attention to how you pay attention, show up and engage. I especially loved the chapter on being aware of your own awareness — it's a simple yet powerful practice. Tricia's voice is big, bold, and all her own — just like this book.

Mari Carmen Pizarro,
Founder and CHRO

In a world where leadership seems obsessed with power and control, Tricia Brouk offers something far more precious: a pathway back to wisdom. Having dedicated my life to helping people rediscover their true selves, I recognize in Tricia's work both a kindred spirit and the kind of leadership our world desperately needs—one that elevates humanity and awakens the best in the human spirit.

Being Smart Is Stupid isn't just another leadership book— it's a restoration manual for leaders who have lost their way in the maze of metrics and manipulation. Tricia's nine principles read like a love letter to the divine wisdom that already exists within each of us.

What moves me most deeply is how Tricia demonstrates that the greatest leaders aren't those who control through manipulation, but those who serve through presence. Her concept of Buddha nature beautifully mirrors what I've witnessed countless times: when we help people reconnect with their inherent wholeness, they become the leaders the world desperately needs.

This book is for every leader who has ever sensed there must be a better way—one that honors both success and the sacred, that builds rather than breaks, that leads from love rather than fear. Tricia shows us that true leadership isn't about becoming smarter; it's about becoming more fully ourselves.

In these pages, you'll rediscover your ability to lead with your heart as well as your head, to see challenges as invitations for growth, and to trust that your deepest wisdom has been there all along, waiting for you to come home to it.

Andrew Bennett,

Founder & President of Bennett Performance Group, Professor at American University, and 2x TEDx Presenter

Tricia Brouk has done a masterful job inviting us into the complexity and beauty of leadership. She teaches us that leadership is less about power and more about presence. *Being Smart is Stupid: Why Embracing the Wisdom of Your Buddha Nature is the Secret to Great Leadership* invites us to quiet the noise, return to our center, and lead from the still, wise place within. It is a gentle yet profound reminder that true influence begins where ego ends and awareness begins.

Alexandra H. Solomon, PhD,

adjunct professor at Northwestern University, bestselling author of *Love Every Day*, and host of the podcast, *Reimagining Love*

CONTENTS

FOREWORD

You interact, but do you inspire? You listen, but do you help? You voice information, but do you say what matters? You reinforce your authority to keep your organization on solid ground, but do you empower others to move mountains?

In a world so often burdened by toxicity and lost potential, your wisdom, empathy, and influence as a leader are desperately needed. The question remains: why do we so often fail to tap into these qualities in our high-tech 21st century?

There's one reason that stands out above all the rest.

We are too smart for our own good.

Having coached many of the world's top leaders over the course of decades, I've had front row seats to the ways in which they make a truly significant impact. What I've seen over and over again is how raw mental calculation is the smallest part of what leads to meaningful work and deep success.

In fact, it often holds us back.

That's why I was so thrilled to encounter Tricia Brouk's book *Being Smart Is Stupid: Why Embracing the Wisdom of Your Buddha*

Nature is the Secret to Great Leadership. While reading, I found myself nodding along with every page.

She has pinpointed the quality the most effective leaders all share.

It is what some of our wisest forebearers dubbed as *Buddha nature.*

The good news is, you possess it as well. This author gives the clearest explanation of it I've encountered anywhere and teaches us all how we can tap into it to build the most amazing life possible.

Tricia Brouk is undoubtedly the right figure to communicate this powerful message. Not only is she an esteemed member of my MG100 Coaches; she is unequivocally the most authentic storyteller and transformer of so many others' authentic stories into their full reception and impact.

Tricia has put thousands of speakers onto big stages across the globe. Sure, brilliance and high creativity play a part, but most importantly, as it relates to this book, her results are intentional, from a nature that we share. To give, to lead. Her primary focus is to create a safe space for her speakers, and that is a space of loving-kindness, authenticity, intention, and listening that lets them speak their truth. They are free. They are empowered.

With this book, Tricia goes much further in her ability to positively influence people and to help them multiply their impact.

I am excited to see what you do with her gift.

-MARSHALL GOLDSMITH
Thinkers50 #1 Executive Coach,
New York Times bestselling author of
The Earned Life, Triggers, and *What Got You Here Won't Get You There.*

INTRODUCTION

When I was seven, I saw my little sister, Jennifer, perform on a huge stage near our tiny hometown of Arnold, Missouri. She was four years old and was tap-dancing in a pink poodle costume. Sitting there in the audience I was overcome by a feeling of certainty that went on to inform the rest of my life.

I was going to dance.

And I was going to be the best dancer in the world.

Of course, there would be no silly poofy dog outfits or corny tap routines for me. I was going to become a ballet dancer. I was going to dance on the biggest stages. I was going to live in New York City.

I begged my parents to enroll me in dance classes at a local studio. When other kids were at the mall or the movies, I was working on my perfect fifth position, grande jetés, and pirouettes. While other kids were watching Saturday morning cartoons, I tuned into PBS, trying to emulate the movements of prima ballerinas like Maya Plisetskaya and Gelsey Kirkland.

My single-minded drive eventually led to my entering a dance competition and winning the title of Petite Jr. Miss Dance of St. Louis at thirteen years old.

The win brought me to the heights of joy.

For about two weeks.

And then I was dissatisfied again.

What did a small city competition mean anyway? The only thing that mattered was getting to New York City. So, I doubled my efforts. More hours spent training. Higher leaps. More pirouettes.

Additional competitions. Bigger awards.

I was more obsessed than ever. I started taking dance classes at the neighboring college in my free time. After the first semester, they offered me a full scholarship to Stephens College, a liberal arts school in Columbia, Missouri, where I could major in dance on an accelerated timeline. That was another moment of certainty.

Before long, I was twenty years old and living in New York City.

I worked with some of the greatest dance companies of our time—Robert Wilson, Big Dance Theater, Pick Up Performance Company, Ben Munisteri Dance, Eun Me Ahn (National Treasure of Korea), and Lucinda Childs (where I danced with Baryshnikov). I was on fire. I was living my dreams. I felt as if all the devotion to mastering every aspect of my art and my craft was in perfect flow.

Not only was I honing my body into a finely tuned machine, but I was honing my mind. My muscle memory was tied to the thousand split-second decisions I made every time I danced. Plus, I masterfully poured over the strategic moves I would make so that I would get to where I wanted to go as efficiently as possible.

And this also meant starting a business so I could make money in between tours. I founded Brouk Moves, an in-home personal training company. I always wanted to have the freedom to dance, make art, and create. I became an entrepreneur so I could make my own rules.

Unlike many other people my age, I understood early that leadership was vital to success—not only leading myself in my dance career, but also my team of trainers inside of Brouk Moves. While I was on tour, my trainers were working with my clients. And eventually, all of my clients were being trained by my team, so that I had the time to start a new company.

I had unrelenting standards. Intense commitment. Unwavering accountability.

I was smart.

And I also experienced suffering.

Now, this isn't to say that I experienced clinical depression or anxiety–conditions with a significant medical component that go well beyond the scope of this book. There were many moments of great happiness and excitement all along the way. To this day, I am grateful that I dedicated myself so fully to dance from such an early age. It gave me experiences I never would have had otherwise and fed my soul as an artist. What's more, a great deal of what I've achieved since those days has been a direct result of the focus, discipline, grit and consistency I learned as a dancer.

What I refer to as suffering could just as easily be called an excess of attachment. I was so completely attached to the outcomes of my efforts that every yes, no, compliment, criticism, step forward, and step back exerted the kind of control over my internal wellbeing that the slightest shift of a rudder does over the direction of a boat.

I was completely unaware of any of this.

I thought I was doing what it took.

I continually obsessed over whether I would land a full-time position with Paul Taylor, Merce Cunningham, Stephen Petronio, or Trisha Brown—one of the great companies that would give me the title of being a "full time dancer with . . ."

When one of my auditions didn't pan out, which happened plenty, I would beat myself up for weeks about how they passed me over.

"This must have been a mistake."

"Maybe they did call my number and I heard it wrong and left the room at the wrong time."

"How could they not want me?"

"Don't they know how hard I work?"

"Don't they realize that I will devote myself to the craft and to being the best in the room?"

"Don't they understand that I am their muse?"

And on top of my ongoing rejections, I had to navigate where I was living. Living in New York City is incredible. But it's not easy. It's expensive, it's loud, it's full of people. I had to find a place to ground. I had to find a place to rest. I had to find a place to center myself in between all of the good, the bad, and the ugly that was my life

Some time during the first half of my twenties, I went searching for an answer.

Having a spiritual practice in what seemed to me to be the most uncertain line of work of all time became remarkably appealing. I hadn't grown up with any organized religion, so I began my search more or less with a blank slate. After exploring various philosophies and reading innumerable books, a professor of mine invited me to a Nichiren Buddhist gathering. There was a click somewhere deep in my heart.

From there, I explored many other branches and schools of Buddhism. The teachings of Vietnamese monk Thich Nhat Hanh resonated particularly deeply with my soul, and I've been immersing myself in his ideas ever since. And I currently have the privilege of studying with Lama Justin Von Bujdoss, who served as the first ever Buddhist chaplain at Rikers Island prison.

I continued to dance all over the world, including the Paris Opera House and Lincoln Center. I've also worked in film, theater, and television with actors like Kate Winslet, Susan Sarandon, Christopher Walken, John Turturro, and James Gandolfini. I've written two musicals, both produced in New York, and have written and directed several successful short documentaries. I've coached former Lieutenant Colonel Alexander Vindman and New York City mayoral candidate Katherine Garcia. And I have even been featured in a documentary called *Big Stages* on Amazon Prime, which is about my second company, The Big Talk, and our work helping thought leaders along their journey to becoming successful speakers.

There's been plenty of joy, but also lots of difficulty. Along the way, I have been sad, jubilant, exalted, and disappointed.

What I no longer do is suffer.

And that has made all the difference.

A few weeks ago, at the time of this writing, a talented playwright I admired invited me to breakfast to discuss her latest project. The script is smart, juicy, and set in the 1970s during the heyday of the women's rights movement. I immediately knew it was exactly the kind of project that excites me most.

I came fully prepared. I had read the play and had taken notes. I made sure the members of my team were holding down the fort so I could rest assured my business was doing fine without me while I focused my attention on this important meeting.

My breakfast date and I had a fantastic conversation about the show's arc and why it was a story that needed to be told. She sensed how well I understood her vision and was, before long, soliciting my ideas. I was armed with the kind of feedback no one else seemed to be giving her.

By the time the check arrived, she was asking me if I'd direct the show.

Naturally, I accepted.

I'd like to say the reason the playwright was so interested in working with me was the extent of my talent, preparation, and ideas. Hopefully, those all played their part. But I truly believe the impression I made—and the result I got—were rooted in the work I've done to practice non-attachment.

During my early days as a dancer, my obsession about the outcome of any encounter would, ironically, result in putting me into a state that made me far less likely to achieve the outcome I wanted so badly. I was completely attached to dancing with Paul Taylor. And every time I got a no, I suffered. For years.

By the time of my recent meeting, I had trained myself to focus wholly on only those parts of the encounter I could control.

My preparation. My work. My ideas.

The world wouldn't collapse no matter what the outcome of the meeting was. And anyway, who was I to judge which outcome was most beneficial for the unfolding of my journey into the future?

My Buddhist practice happens to be the tool that allows me to maintain my equilibrium in the midst of a life that many might see as overloaded, chaotic, and intense. However, this is in no way a book about why you should become a Buddhist.

For millennia, countless human beings have wrestled with their own versions of the issues I've described above. They have had a vision for how they wanted their lives to unfold and a determination to wrestle the world around them into that shape.

The problem with this approach is manifold. For one, it makes life incredibly painful, even if—sometimes precisely because—you succeed. More than this, though, tying your internal wellbeing to the achievement of a specific outcome requires at least some degree of pushing, pulling, strategizing, quantifying, manipulating, or cajoling to get you there. If only one outcome is acceptable, there is no other option but to force the people and the environment that surrounds you into compliance.

In most professional circles, this sort of force of will is considered "smart."

And it often does get people at least some of their desired results in the short term. In the long run, however, it will inevitably fracture your foundational long-term relationships and ecosystem as if you were trying to cram a delicate ceramic plate into an overstuffed China cabinet.

Long-term success requires leadership. Great leadership has very little to do with your ability to impress people with your skills. And it certainly has nothing to do with how smart you are.

Smart vs. Wise

Since the ascendance of the internet economy, there has arisen an obsession with being smart.

In his book *In the Plex: How Google Thinks, Works, and Shapes Our Lives*, technology journalist Steven Levy reported that Google cofounder Sergey Brin "doesn't trust people who he thinks don't approach his level of intelligence."

Jeff Bezos built Amazon, his "Everything Store," largely through an obsessive focus on the productivity metrics of every aspect of his operation.

And Elon Musk, perhaps the most famous of the new breed of smart leaders, is known to publicly berate employees who give him answers he deems not up to the intellectual clarity he demands. In fact, he is so obsessed with this worldview that he regularly tells the press of his plan to populate the planet with more smart people like himself, which accounts for his fourteen different children with four different women.

Now, I'm not going to try to claim that founders, executives, and managers with high IQs never build big things, make a lot of money, or accumulate large followings of people who hang on their every word.

Still, it's worth asking if it's worth it.

Zuckerberg's Facebook, and the other social media platforms he's acquired or built, are now widely considered to be such a danger to the mental health of young people that the Surgeon General issued a rare public warning about them.

One of the warehouse workers was fired by Jeff Bezos's hyper-quantified company because he protested inadequate safety measures that would have impacted speed of delivery ended up organizing one of the first major labor unions to arise since the Industrial Revolution. It has become a major hitch in Bezos's plans for total world domination.

And Musk—well, we see the results of his approach virtually every day. The bizarre public comments. The strange acquisition and evisceration of the once-mighty Twitter. The trans daughter who doesn't talk to him.

Add to this list Elizabeth Holmes, the fraudulent Theranos founder who went to prison for her smart scheme.

All of these people are different in their goals and so-called achievements, but what they have in common is that they are driven by a relentless craving. Each of them is characterized by a gnawing dissatisfaction constantly shouting at them that if they don't get what they want, they will lose all worth as human beings.

As such, they berate, manipulate, and coldly optimize everyone around them. They interact with their employees, their partners, their spouses, and their children as if they were chess pieces on a board that they can ultimately maneuver into the right position as long as they apply enough brain power.

The result is pervasive anxiety, high turnover, low morale, burnout, and severed relationships at every turn.

Apparently, it isn't sufficient to simply be smart.

Then, what's the alternative?

Is there a better framework for understanding what healthy, adaptive, sustainable leadership might look like?

Yes, there is.

Wisdom.

The philosophy I was fortunate enough to encounter early in my adult life is often referred to as a "wisdom tradition," but it is not the only one. The Sufi tradition in Islam, Jewish Kabbalah, certain forms of Christian monasticism, and some types of what people often refer to as New Age thought, all contain seeds of what I'm referring to.

Many people have come to this alternate worldview without the aid of an established tradition.

Whatever the path you might take to get there, there is no escaping one universal truth.

Cultivating wisdom is essential for truly effective leadership.

Cultivating leadership is essential for a good life in general.

The Other Side of the Story

Okay, now here's where you might be saying to yourself something like: "That all sounds well and good to be a 'wise' leader. But it seems a little disconnected from reality to me. We're in business here. Wisdom is nice when you're sitting on top of a mountain, but business is about cash flow and profits."

This is a common enough point of view, but it's a lie.

It's a lie propagated by the business media and countless self-congratulatory business biographies.

Even if you are willing to sleep under your desk six nights a week, come to work every day knowing your entire team despises you, and alienate your friends and family, I hope to convince you that emphasizing smarts over wisdom will mean that whatever success you have will inevitably be short term. All the while, you'll be fostering an army of sycophants who will sabotage you at the closest opportunity. I don't mean to scare you. I do mean to inspire you to think differently about your leadership and success.

Moreover, despite whatever money you make, you will find yourself shackled to what you've built. Emotionally and mentally, if not financially and physically, your feverish attachments to your goals will lead you to where they want you to go rather than you having the freedom to use your goals in service of the life you desire.

Richard Branson has founded many companies, some which were unparalleled successes and others that have been shuttered. But all who know him say that his drive never eclipses his sense of play. And his business never eclipses his relationships. From the beginning of his professional life, he had his kids around the office. Those who didn't like it were free to move on. And his thirty-five year-long marriage is the stuff of Hollywood movies.

Wisdom.

During the late-nineties dot-com boom, investors and pundits lambasted Warren Buffet for having finally lost his touch. He was still investing in companies like Coca-Cola while all the young, sophisticated financial wizards were making mountains of money in the new digital economy. None of this phased Buffet one bit. At a famous investors conference, he held up a can of Coke (which he still drinks regularly at ninety-plus years old) and said, "I understand this product. I'm not so sure about the other stuff."

When 1999 rolled around, all the young investors went broke, and the Oracle of Omaha made more money than ever before.

Wisdom.

In an age where people said no one was reading anymore, daytime talk show host Oprah Winfrey created Oprah's Book Club. It offered challenging, thoughtful novels like *Beloved* by Toni Morrison and William Faulkner's *As I Lay Dying*, along with more contemporary works of literary fiction. Critics mocked the idea that anyone but the smallest core of intellectuals in America would read anything beyond airport thrillers and romance novels.

A few years later, Oprah's Book Club was arguably the single most important force in publishing.

Wisdom.

Although few, if any, of these leaders are technically Buddhists, we have a name for tapping into this kind of wisdom to set an example for others and shape the universe in a way that brings benefit to both you and anyone who crosses your path.

This is ... *Leading from your Buddha Nature.*

How To Use This Book

Nobody ever said leading from a place of wisdom is easy.

It certainly wasn't easy for me to learn.

I put my mind to it because I knew living a life with constant suffering was not the life I wanted to live.

I experimented with countless different approaches until I found what worked for me. Then I compared my approach with what other great leaders I admired had done. Finally, I refined my approach by using it with my clients.

And above all I practiced. And practiced. And practiced.

Just like in ballet. I did the pliés.

This book is the culmination of a near lifetime of that practice.

Unlike many books that you can dip into and out of at various places, *Being Smart Is Stupid* is meant to be read in order. Each chapter is contingent upon the one before it. It isn't just a typical leadership manual filled with quick tips or isolated tactics. The structure of the book is deliberately designed to build upon itself, meaning that each chapter is part of a larger journey toward embracing wisdom-based leadership.

It is worthwhile to read the book from beginning to end. However, nothing will change for you if that's all you do. To use this book in a way that will affect real change in your life, your work, and the quality and effectiveness of your leadership, you must practice and internalize the concepts as you go, getting one into your bones before moving onto the next.

The earliest chapters in the book lay the groundwork. They teach basic concepts and exercises that will immediately allow you to see reality with a clarity that has likely eluded you. The techniques and frameworks provided in these early chapters are simple, but certainly not easy, to master. They also dissect the limitations of ego-driven leadership and explore the downsides of relying solely on cold intellect to lead.

As we progress, the book will dig deep into the concept of cultivating your Buddha nature and explain how it contrasts with the ego nature. Then I'll provide you with practical tools and exercises to help you gradually let go of your attachment to being "smart" and to help you start cultivating wisdom in your leadership.

From there, we will focus on deepening the practice of wisdom-based leadership, exploring how you can incorporate these ideas into your daily decision-making and interactions with your team. We'll also cover tactical practices for fostering calm, creativity, and collaboration in an organization by embracing your Buddha nature and detaching from ego-driven impulses.

Finally, we will go into higher-level, "advanced" concepts like practicing impermanence, recognizing oneness, and becoming aware of awareness.

You'll come away from this book with a radically new framing of what it means to lead effectively that is as ancient as the dawn of time and as current and relevant as your latest team meeting.

Chapter 1

GET STILL

In the summer of 1940, the German Luftwaffe launched a relentless bombing campaign across the major cities of Great Britain. Defeat seemed likely. The Third Reich had, only months earlier, rolled its tanks over Western Europe and conquered most of it in six weeks. The British army, attempting to defend its allies in France, suffered a humiliating defeat on the beaches of Dunkirk—their soldiers' survival ultimately depending on an improbable rescue by small commercial vessels and fishing boats. The British people were terrified, demoralized, and battered by loss and sorrow.

As you might imagine, Prime Minister Winston Churchill was under a lot of pressure.

He was required to make more life-or-death decisions every day than most of us will make over an entire lifetime. He had to somehow bolster the morale of his nation in the face of unimaginable horror and uncertainty. He had to coordinate efforts with foreign allies ranging from the United States to the Soviet Union.

Somehow, facing nearly impossible odds, Churchill led his country to stave off the German invasion. And from there, Britain and its allies went on to win the war.

How did he accomplish this incredible feat?

Did the leader of the United Kingdom work without pause, racing relentlessly from emergency to emergency, barking orders at underlings who didn't understand the importance of their mission?

No.

Winston Churchill took naps.

Each afternoon, as bombs rained down on London, the Prime Minister retired to his specially-appointed fortified underground room and slept for an hour or two. His staff knew not to bother him. They understood that during this time, he was off-limits.

It's hard to believe. Not only does this image of Churchill in his pajamas snoozing during the middle of the day clash with most peoples' image of a wartime leader; it clashes with the image of any successful leader at all.

Of course, when it comes to powerful leaders, we're typically more likely to think of Elon Musk sleeping for only two hours a night *total* under his desk at the Tesla factory. Or maybe some of us picture Steve Jobs screaming at his employees for failing to develop a fast enough iPhone processor in time for the holiday season. Or Amy Klobuchar throwing binders at staff members. Or Simon Cowell turning American Idol contestants into quivering masses of self-loathing as he crushes their dreams.

But shouldn't leaders always grind harder, push further, and never ever settle for anything less than the very best?

Not so, according to consultant Alex Soojung-Kim Pang. "Not only did a nap help Churchill keep up his energy," Pang wrote in his 2018 book *Rest: Why You Get More Done When You Work Less,* "his sangfroid also inspired his cabinet and officers. Napping during boring parliamentary debates was one thing. Going to sleep literally while bombs were falling signaled Churchill's confidence in his staff and his belief that the dark days would pass."

It's a far cry from the adrenaline-jacked hustle culture we've all become used to seeing everywhere we turn.

However, when I read about Churchill's strategy, it stood out to me as an indication of a far deeper wisdom than someone who simply knew how to stay sharp and recharge his batteries. In fact, it struck me as being highly aligned with a powerful insight I myself have gained from my many years of Buddhist practice.

Winston Churchill understood the importance of getting still.

If Churchill Could Tap into His Buddha Nature, You Can Too

Although most of us don't have to lead a beleaguered nation against a once-in-a-millennium military assault, we all encounter stresses, conflicts, and roadblocks that can feel like the end of the world. If you're like so many of the leaders I cross paths with, you spend a lot of your time "putting out fires." Perhaps this takes the form of having to manage difficult clients, employees who never seem to learn from their mistakes, or back-to-back meetings and calls that keep you from getting any real work done.

A lot of us simply resign ourselves to our fates, bouncing around like pinballs from workplace emergency to workplace emergency until we collapse at the end of the day. Others of us battle to become more proactive about improving focus and performance.

As for this second group, an entire industry has arisen to serve them.

A rash of corporate wellness programs have sprung up, focusing on both the body and mind. These range from in-office workshops to multi-day offsite retreats. Many of them feature instruction on mindfulness meditation.

Aiming to optimize efficiency and productivity, the new mindfulness meditation gurus tend to prescribe a fairly intensive discipline. They often recommend that clients start their days with a twenty-plus-minute silent meditation session first thing in the morning, sitting cross-legged on specially-designed cushions. They provide intricate lessons on how to focus on the breath. For the particularly ambitious, sessions are regularly paired with cold plunges and journaling marathons.

Don't get me wrong, I'm a big believer in meditation. I have a robust practice of my own. I've even attended, and enjoyed, a meditation retreat or two in my time. I'm also a big proponent of cultivating mental focus and, for that matter, making profits in business.

Where I do see a problem, however, is when we separate the practice of getting still from the rest of our lives.

You already have a Buddha nature, whether you regularly attend sponsored ten-day silent meditation retreats or not. The trick is quieting yourself down enough to get in touch with it.

We tend to worship Abraham Lincoln as our great national hero, but those close to him knew how crushing his experience in the White House often was. Throughout his presidency, he was beset on all sides by criticism, danger, and incompetence as he tried to keep the Union together during the Civil War. He was lambasted in the press, subjected to multiple assassination attempts, and regularly disrespected in public by his Cabinet members.

More than anything, he was subjected to utter ineptness and disregard by his own generals. Before he found and promoted

Ulysses S. Grant, those entrusted with leading his army botched the job at critical moments over and over again.

The worst of these instances was when General George Meade, after overseeing a pivotal victory at the Battle of Gettysburg, failed to pursue Confederate General Robert E. Lee—a mistake that extended the war unnecessarily by another two years.

President Lincoln understood the gravity of this mistake as soon as he heard of it, and he was despondent.

Many of us, if we were in his place, would have probably summoned the general, berated him, and immediately fired him—at minimum. And Lincoln's first impulse was to do just that. It certainly would have made him feel better—for a moment or two, at least. But then he would have been left without anyone to lead the Union forces, and his setback would have become exponentially more serious.

Instead, he wrote a letter.

The letter talked about how the horrible aftermath of Gettysburg was completely Meade's fault. It called him out for his terrible blunder. It excoriated him for his incompetence and blamed the inevitable extension of the war on him and him alone.

Once he finished writing it, the President put the letter in a drawer and sealed the envelope.

He never sent it.

Abraham Lincoln was a very smart man. He devoured books, learned the legal profession on his own while living on the frontier, and wrote prose that rivaled that of the best poets and novelists of his time.

None of this is what makes a majority of historians consider him to be the best President in American history.

Abraham Lincoln's success as a leader came from his wisdom.

Unlike the 170-ton Lincoln Memorial statue in Washington D.C., the real Abraham Lincoln was a human being. The prospect of failing in his duty obsessed him with worry. In private, he often came to the edge of exploding.

He knew all of this about himself. To mitigate it, he developed and built-in a nonnegotiable stillness practice. He learned how to put a beat between stimulus and response.

Writing letters he never sent was a perfect example of this.

The simple act of getting his thoughts out on paper stilled his automatic emotions. After that, he would be able to calculate the wisest, most strategic course of action most likely to help him achieve the goals he needed to achieve.

Even the wisest among us sometimes react instead of responding. To combat this all-too-human tendency, establish your own version of the daily nap or the unsent letter policy. In your case, it might be that you always take three deep breaths before answering any difficult question. Or maybe you make it a practice to step into the next room and then back in again when an employee messes up an important task.

Whatever you choose, figuring it out in advance, and practicing the habit when smaller challenges arise, will help you ensure that when truly big problems come up, your own ego-based tendencies won't betray you.

The Science of Stillness

When we act without first getting still, what happens in our brains?

The work of Daniel J. Siegel, a clinical psychiatrist, professor, and researcher who has studied the primal biological roots of behavior, provides some answers.

In his book *Mindsight*, Siegel writes about the structure of the human brain as composed of several distinct areas that each developed during different periods of our evolutionary heritage. The oldest part of our brains is the limbic area, which we share with lizards, fish, and frogs.

As Siegel describes it, the limbic area "creates not only our basic drives but also our emotions . . . 'Is this good or is this bad?' is the most basic question the limbic area addresses. We move toward the good and withdraw from the bad."

Although the limbic area is ancient, it is also incredibly important. Just as a lizard will bolt at a loud noise or the appearance of a cat, our limbic areas make us run away from—or fight against—sources of danger and move toward sources of pleasure. The limbic area keeps us alive. If we had to go through a philosophical back and forth about whether to slam on the brakes every time a car driving close to us ran a red light, we wouldn't last long.

However, we don't realize we are experiencing different kinds of events with different parts of our brains. We operate under the illusion that we have one self that makes decisions in the same way every time. That's true for unwise decisions as well as wise ones. When we experience primal anger and chew out a team member who makes a mistake, we rationalize it to ourselves afterwards. When we jump on the chance to sign a deal that doesn't align with the values of our business because it will bring in *so much* money, we justify it later with the aid of income statements, balance sheets, and convoluted interpretations of our mission-and-value statements.

This tendency gets even more dangerous when our present is colored by negative experiences from our past.

As Siegel explains, "traumatic experiences, in particular, can sensitize limbic reactivity, so that even minor stresses can cause cortisol to spike, making daily life more challenging for the traumatized person."

There may be a lot of disagreement in our public discourse right now as to what qualifies as "trauma." But as far as the brain is concerned, most of us won't escape without experiencing one or more traumatic experiences during our lifetimes. It is, unfortunately, a facet of being human.

Have you ever had an experience where someone at work makes a seemingly innocuous comment and you respond in a way which in hindsight you know didn't match the offense? Maybe it was a small joke or poorly chosen word. And you react by snapping at them, going ice cold, or a combination of both.

This is your maladaptive limbic area in action.

Unfortunately, by the time of adulthood, all of our limbic areas are maladaptive in one way or another.

The good news is that we can counteract the effects of the reptile brain. "Finding a way to soothe excessively reactive limbic firing is crucial to rebalancing emotions and diminishing the harmful effects of chronic stress," writes Siegel, "[we can] recruit the higher areas of the brain to create a 'cortical override' of these limbic reactivities."

"Imagine a peaceful river running through the countryside," Dr. Siegel elaborates in his book *The Whole-Brain Child*, "That's the river of your well-being. Whenever you're in the water, peacefully floating along in your canoe, you feel like you're generally in a good relationship with the world around you. You have a clear understanding of yourself, other people, and your life. You can be flexible and adjust when situations change. You're stable and at peace."

He then goes on to describe the river's two banks. One of the banks, he writes, represents chaos—which is the feeling of being completely out of control, as demonstrated by impulsivity, aggression, and thoughtlessness. The other bank represents rigidity, which is a state in which "you become completely unwilling to adapt, compromise, or negotiate."

We often spend much of our lives skirting one bank or the other, or bouncing and lurching between the two. But what Siegel posits is that we can learn to engage in practices that integrate the various upper and lower parts of our brain, and by so doing, spend most of our time floating down the middle of the river.

And what does he prescribe for doing so?

He encourages us to create a space between the triggering activity and our reaction to it.

In other words, what the doctor prescribes is *getting still*.

How to Do It: The STILL Method

Although the specific details of how to get still can and should vary, there are certain broad principles that always apply. I describe them below in an acronym (sometimes I can be a little cheesy, please forgive me) to help you remember it.

Stop— Literally stop what you are doing. This is by far the most challenging of all the steps that I'm asking you to implement when it comes to becoming truly wise. It feels so good in the moment to keep talking, keep arguing, keep defending, keep reacting, and keep acting. That's what smart people do, right? But when we don't take a pause first, our egos (and our limbic areas) take over.

Tune In—Once you've stopped, you have the space to tune in. This means asking yourself, "What are the emotions I'm feeling right now? What am I feeling about the person I'm facing? What do I want to do right now?" Without judgment or attachment, simply notice. And remember what you are experiencing is an emotion. It says nothing about who you are.

Intuit—At this point, you'll know what to do and what needs to happen without the need for rational, fact-based analysis. This is your intuition kicking in. Take it seriously. It comes from the truest part of yourself—your Buddha nature.

Listen—Once you've established your intuition, listen to it. When you do, you'll receive the guidance you need for your next step. If you feel uneasy in your body and heart, even though there's not yet a logical explanation as to why, it's time to take a pause. Put off that decision. Do not engage in that tough conversation. On the other hand, if you feel calm and solid, even if the situation is uncertain, it's time to act.

Learn—The more you stop, tune in, intuit and listen, you'll learn how to cultivate the practice of getting still. And getting still gives you the space to learn from the experience. Ask yourself whether you've arrived at the place where you can cultivate the ability to respond and not react. If not, stay curious, keep practicing, keep learning. It's an ongoing process.

Constructive Rest

One of the earliest techniques I discovered for proactively cultivating stillness came through my youthful journey to relentlessly improve my dance technique. During this time, I discovered a method called the Alexander Technique's Constructive Rest.

It can be done in just a few minutes from practically anywhere and will serve as a sort of reset button in the midst of an upsurge of triggering pressure or stress, as it releases the tension stored in your body.

Getting Started: Choose a clean, firm, and comfortable surface—ideally the floor, which provides stable support. If lying directly on the floor feels awkward, try a carpet, towel, or folded blanket.

Lie on your back with your head supported by a few books or yoga blocks, adjusting the height until your neck feels supported yet soft. Bend your knees and keep your feet flat on the floor. Rest your arms with your hands on your torso.

Expanding Awareness: Allow your mind to settle. Relax your gaze, noticing the space at the edges of your vision. Rather than focusing outward, let the room's light come to you.

Keep your eyes level above your cheekbones. Gradually widen your awareness to include the room around you as well as your own body. Instead of concentrating on your body, let its sensations gently come into your awareness.

When your mind wanders, bring it back to the present, focusing on the ceiling with awareness centered behind your eyes.

Observing the Body: Notice where your body meets the floor. Sense areas that feel compressed or tight, noting places where tension resides.

Releasing Tension: As you observe, practice letting go of tension you don't need. If some areas still hold tension, allow them to remain as they are.

Find the minimum effort needed to keep your knees in position without them drifting. If they do drift, gently bring them back toward the ceiling.

Guiding Your Body: Without checking for changes, send a mental message to your neck to release and allow your head to rest easily away from the top of your spine. Imagine your back widening and lengthening, your knees extending toward the ceiling, and your shoulders softening outward.

Notice the rhythm of your breath, following each exhale naturally without changing it. Let each inhale come without actively drawing it in.

Returning to the Day: When you're ready to get up, pause before moving. Reconnect with the sense of expanded awareness and use it as part of your rising process. Once standing, pause once more.

Allow your neck to release. Imagine your torso becoming tall and broad, your knees pointing forward with ease, and your shoulders widening. Do this without actively checking for changes—then continue with your day.

Applying Stillness in the Real World

I find it incredible that a philosopher who we now call the Buddha worked out how we humans can cultivate wise decision-making in our own lives two-thousand-plus years before anyone on earth knew anything about the biology of the brain.

I find it equally fascinating that various great leaders throughout history figured out their own methods for hacking the most primitive parts of their brains to gain access to unlimited sources of wisdom.

While many of the specific strategies we've discussed are useful, each person will need to tailor their approach for getting still to their own personality, preferences, and life practices.

What often makes it so difficult to find stillness is that it pushes against the oldest and more primal parts of ourselves.

The solution is to start small.

You might be stuck in traffic when you need to find stillness. Or maybe you're in the middle of Times Square. Perhaps you're trying to take an important call while your kids are running around you and screaming. These, not when you've blocked off ten days to go to a meditation retreat in the countryside, are the times that truly require us to build in stillness practices. These are the times when consciously placing a space between stimulus and response will make all the difference.

Create an escape hatch—a plausible "excuse" to take yourself into a new setting momentarily. Build in non-negotiables, which, by the time a truly challenging situation arises, everyone will already accept as part of your way of doing business. Come up with ways to calm your mind in advance.

With a little bit of creativity, you can set up opportunities to avail yourself of stillness, well before the need occurs.

Wrapping It Up

Carve out your non-negotiables. Whether it's a daily nap or a night of sleep before having to make a decision, establish these boundaries and communicate them firmly.

Create delays between stimulus and response. Maybe it's a separate email address where you forward angry emails before deciding whether to really send them or not. Perhaps it's a three count before answering. It's essential to decide on this before challenging interactions occur and then work on building the habit.

Steer down the middle of the river. Do you notice yourself flying off the handle when challenging situations arise? Do you become stuck in your ways and inflexible? Or do you bounce between the two extremes? Understand that this is a human tendency and take solace that incorporating stillness will help you better navigate them.

Establish a physical practice. Whether it's the Alexander Technique, yoga, or long walks, getting out of your chair makes it easier to get still.

Practice the Get STILL method – Stop, Tune In, Intuit, Listen, Learn.

Start small. The time to rely on getting still after a lifetime of noisy reactivity is not when you have a major crisis on your hands. Find low-risk, low-impact opportunities in your day to work on these strategies so that you'll have them at your disposal when you really need them.

Build habits. Just because you understand the importance of creating space between stimulus and response, tuning into what your mind and heart are telling you, and responding rather than reacting, that doesn't make it easy. Learning to truly get still is like learning to play an instrument—only, in this case, the instrument is you.

A few guiding questions to help you access your Buddha nature:

1. What are the stimuli that might come up in your life that have the most potential to activate the least wise parts of yourself?

2. What are your non-negotiables? Think them through here in advance so you'll already be prepared when life or work gets stressful.

_____

_____

_____

_____

3. What is one small stillness strategy you can commit to practicing first?

_____

_____

_____

_____

Chapter 2

EMBODY GRATITUDE

Ever since Indra Nooyi left India to attend the Yale School of Management in the late 1970s, she had worked nonstop. Her first job after graduating was at Johnson & Johnson, where she quickly distinguished herself as a project manager. Soon she was hired as a strategic consultant at BCG, where her performance attracted the attention of major players both within and beyond the consulting industry.

From there, Nooyi moved to Motorola, where she served as both Director of Corporate Strategy & Planning and Senior Vice President. Next, it was a stint at the multibillion-dollar multinational electrical engineering company Asea Brown Boveri.

By the mid 1990s, food and beverage conglomerate PepsiCo had added this star recruit to its roster. She rocketed through the ranks—moving from Senior Vice President to Chief Financial Officer for the entire company in only seven years.

Finally, in 2006, Indra Nooyi was appointed CEO—only the fifth in PepsiCo's history and the first woman to ever hold the position.

Before her new duties began in earnest, she took a short trip home to see her family, unsure of when she would be able to do so again in light of her very busy, very important schedule.

Maybe she was expecting a hometown hero's welcome.

If so, she was in for a surprise.

During an appearance on the popular business podcast The David Rubenstein Show, Nooyi described what happened instead. As she sat in the living room of the house where she had grown up, people began to arrive—some of whom she knew and a lot of whom she didn't.

Not one of them gave her more than a brisk greeting.

They were there to see her mother.

"They'd go to my mom," she explained, "and say, 'You did such a good job with your daughter. Compliments to you. She's CEO.'"

If she had grown up somewhere else, the experience might have been a blow to her ego. Instead, it caused her to reflect.

It occurred to her, as if for the first time, that despite her hard work and focus, she did have her parents to thank for her success. When she was a little girl, her mother had her and her sister write and present speeches about what they would do as world leaders. She would create games to teach them how to get better at strategy. She, and Nooyi's father who had died a few years earlier, had dedicated their lives to their children.

Nooyi now saw clearly that her achievements were the result of that dedication.

If her parents had been so pivotal to her accomplishments, she thought, what about the parents of the talented and driven senior executives she relied on every day?

Not long after she arrived back in the States, Nooyi began to write letters. She wrote to the parents of all the executives who reported directly to her. She described to them the specific contributions their kids were making at PepsiCo. She ended every letter with the words: "Thank you for the gift of your child to our company."

The effect was nearly immediate—and dramatic.

First, she received a flood of joyfully surprised responses from the parents she had sent her letters to. Next, the executives themselves approached her. Their veneer of polish dropped as they told her how this was one of the most significant events in their parents' lives, which made it one of the most significant events in their own lives.

What had started as a spontaneous expression of gratitude turned into a regular practice. Throughout her tenure as PepsiCo CEO between 2006-2018, Indra Nooyi wrote roughly 400 letters each year to the parents of high-performing executives throughout the organization.

It is almost certainly no coincidence that Nooyi's approval rating within the organization, as assessed through anonymous company-wide reviews, was a consistent 75%. Moreover, during her time at the company's helm, PepsiCo's annual net profit increased from $2.7 billion to $6.5 billion.

The Perils of Performative Gratitude

It is no secret that expressing gratitude is supposed to be good for you—and good for business. A study by Quantum Research Workplace, for instance, found that employees are 2.7 times more likely to be highly engaged when they find their contributions are genuinely recognized. Another study by psychologist Roger Emmons, PhD at the University of California, Davis found that gratitude "lowers the stress response ... [and] can reduce cortisol levels—the primary stress hormone—by up to 23%."

Findings like these have made gratitude hot, and there is no shortage of professional advice purporting to teach ambitious leaders how to capitalize on it.

Take the popularity of the gratitude journal. A quick glance at any airport bookstore or LinkedIn feed will feature some version of a commandment for readers to write down three things they are grateful for every day (often, for some reason, in a Moleskine notebook, which costs about three times more than the typical legal pad).

In some circles, "I appreciate you" has replaced "it was nice to meet you" as a standard conversation closer, even when the people in question barely know each other.

Gift cards from Starbucks and Target have become to cubicle-farms what cigarettes once were in prisons.

In short, the business world has come to view "gratitude" as a *smart* business strategy.

It is these sorts of surface-level displays that I call *performative gratitude*—the strategic deployment of gratitude to get a certain result.

It's the gratitude leaders think they *should* engage in.

Human beings are highly attuned to the nuances of inter-personal interactions. Consider how we can tell whether someone is happy or sad based only on a few millimeters difference in the position of their mouth or eyes. Most of this happens on the sub-conscious level. We are constantly scanning for and picking up on micro-expressions and behavioral inconsistencies to decide whether someone we are interacting with is trustworthy and genuine. It helped our ancestors survive in the wild and it helps us survive in the workplace.

As a result, the benefits of performative gratitude only last for so long. People inevitably see through self-motivated displays of gratitude.

There is another way.

Katannuta is a word in Pali, the language spoken by the original Buddha, which literally means "to have a sense of what was done." It corresponds roughly with our English word "gratitude" but encompasses a great deal more. It is considered one of the main cornerstones of what Buddhists refer to as enlightenment, encompassing mindfulness, the interconnectedness of all living creatures, compassion, and the full opening of one's heart to others with whom we share the world.

In short, it is *embodying* gratitude rather than *expressing* gratitude.

I know there's a good chance you're thinking right now that this all seems a little bit pie-in-the-sky. You're just looking to keep your team excited about what they do every day so that they perform well, while keeping yourself sane in the process.

I get it, but bear with me.

Throughout the rest of this chapter, I'm going to attempt to break down this concept into down-to-earth terms that are relevant to the challenges we encounter in the modern workplace. In short, we're looking to replace the empty gestures of performative gratitude with something more meaningful, heartfelt, and, ultimately, effective.

Some of the most successful leaders have transformed their lives and their organizations by harnessing the power of Katannuta—or embodied gratitude— even if they don't know it by name. By examining their example, we can begin to do the same.

The Embodiment of Gratitude

In 2014, Whitney Wolfe Herd was fired from Tinder—an organization she helped create.

As one of the cofounders of the company that more or less kicked off the dating app craze, Wolfe Herd worked backbreaking hours at a mind-scrambling pace. She effectively suspended her social life. She compulsively jolted out of bed each night every two hours to check her email, before falling back into a light sleep. She put everything else on hold in deference to the company.

It was unclear to most everybody why Wolfe Herd was fired. By all reports, she has a brilliant mind and was an excellent leader and team member. She was the person most responsible for building the company's brand to the extent that, at a certain point, the word "Tinder" was nearly synonymous with online dating.

Not long after she was unceremoniously pushed out, she filed a lawsuit. It claimed that she was sexually harassed during her time at Tinder.

The case was eventually settled, but not before she was blasted with a relentless barrage of vitriol courtesy of the same internet ecosystem in which she had made her name.

During an interview on the Tim Ferriss Show, Wolfe Herd had the following to say about this time in her life: "[One] piece painted me as this Gone Girl of tech. She was a seductress and blah, blah, and all of these awful insinuations. And it was talking about ridiculous things like really personal details that were completely inaccurate . . . And that was what was so devastating. My dad was just like—having your father send you an article and being like is this true, of course no. But how do you justify that at twenty-four, just turning twenty-five years old, to your father."

Wolfe Herd plunged into despondency. Already prone to anxiety, she suffered what she termed as a mental breakdown and what clinicians called a "clinical panic attack"—hyperventilation, loss of breath, and nausea.

Eventually, she pulled herself out of the crisis by doing what she did best. She founded another company, this time with her calling the shots.

When she came up with the idea for Bumble—a dating app where only women make the first move—Wolfe Herd almost certainly knew she had hit upon a blockbuster idea. However, a lot of blockbuster ideas fail. What allowed her to build the kind of organization that would eventually facilitate the new app's fantastic success was her commitment to embodying the opposite of what she experienced at Tinder.

In describing her new worldview in a 2017 interview, Wolfe Herd said, "Everyone who touches your company or brand, you should be so grateful that they are dedicating their time, their knowledge, and their skills to something you created . . . Sometimes it's just a little bit backwards. People feel that people should be lucky to work for them."

Wolfe Herd designed every aspect of the company as an extension of this sentiment. For example, "The Hive"—Bumble's headquarters—offers private spaces for nursing mothers and manicures on Fridays. Parents are allowed to bring their children to the office when they need to. Employees receive reimbursements for gym memberships and are encouraged to leave work to take care of time-sensitive errands and medical appointments.

These are no mere perks. The intention comes from a very different place than the tech startup foosball tables and beer kegs once deployed with the intention of recruiting "rockstar" talent and discouraging them from ever leaving the office once they're hooked. What Wolfe Herd set out to do was to create a workplace that reflected gratitude for her team in every facet.

Breaking into the online dating space so late in the game was a difficult undertaking. At the time, Match.com had already created a near monopoly through its acquisition of the biggest players in the space, including OkCupid, PlentyofFish, Hinge, and, of course, Tinder.

Yet, despite having been founded after almost all of these industry leaders, Bumble exploded. At the time of this writing, the company is worth $1 billion with 50 million users in 190 countries. It has become the single most downloaded dating app in the United States.

Embodying gratitude as a leader, as Whitney Wolfe Herd's story attests, means dedicating the time, energy, curiosity, and willingness to develop a profound understanding of why you are grateful for your team, as well as for the opportunity to do what you do.

When you rely on mere displays of performative gratitude, like the corny gift card given during the holidays (or, of course, display no gratitude at all), your team might actually start sabotaging your initiatives, even if they do so unintentionally. Over the long run, it is incredibly difficult to run a successful organization without trust, and gratitude is the foundation of trust.

In short, if you're using gratitude as a tool or tactic, it's not gratitude. Leaders who embody gratitude aren't doing so to achieve a tit-for-tat ROI. They're doing it because it's the wise thing to do, and they understand that everything else will follow from that.

That said, cultivating and communicating embodied gratitude will deliver an unbelievable return on investment in the long run. Your team members will become proactive. They'll begin solving problems without you having to ask them to because they will feel valued and seen. It is, in many ways, the most effective and affordable team-building methodology leaders can invest in.

But it doesn't always come naturally.

Human beings tend to focus on the negative rather than the positive. It's a tendency that probably helped our cave-ancestors survive. These days, however, it can lead to some seriously nasty consequences.

If you ignore all the good your team members—not to mention friends, partners, and loved ones—are doing, but seize on every tiny mistake with a battery of criticism and vitriol, you won't have many team members, friends, partners, or loved ones for very long.

What's the antidote? How can we trick ourselves—or train ourselves—out of this encoded aspect of human nature?

Instead of simply telling yourself you *should* be more grateful, focus on *why* you might feel grateful.

For example, let's say you have an executive assistant who is fantastic at sorting through your emails to make sure you only have to deal personally with those that are high-priority or require a timely response. Performative gratitude would have you give this assistant a card every holiday season along with the same gift certificate you give to everyone else on your team. But imagine if you first thought deeply about *why* this ability to serve as a shield between you and a relentless flood of emails was so valuable.

Perhaps then you'd realize that by doing such a good job at screening emails, your assistant effectively gave you an additional block of uninterrupted time every day that you used to do the deep work which led to the innovations that gave your company its most profitable quarter in five years. It could be that you would be overwhelmed with a surge of true gratitude where before there was just a sense of expectation.

From this starting place, gestures of embodied gratitude become inevitable. And from embodied gratitude, truly wise leadership—and all the results that come with it—will grow.

From the Files of Tricia Brouk:

I recently attended the 40 Years of Zen retreat, which bills itself as an "immersive neurofeedback experience" that lets attendees "access the benefits of forty years of meditation in five days." The program came well recommended, aligned with my interests, and I was too curious not to check it out. Still, there are a lot of programs out there making a lot of claims and I came to this one with a skeptical mind. Turns out, it delivered on its promises and more.

Throughout the week I experienced group integration sessions, nootropic supplement immersion, and training in biohacking. It was pretty wild. Above all, however, it was the neurofeedback sessions that made the biggest impact on me.

The idea was that I'd practice deep gratitude every day. Then, at a certain point, I would enter into a dark pod and attach to a device that would scan my brain waves for changes.

On the first day, my gamma brainwaves—the ones asso-ciated with intuition and manifestation—appeared to be in a range that was pretty standard for a normal human being. And that means they appeared to be very low on the scale—relatively inactive. However, as I continued to focus on embodying gratitude each day, these gamma brain-waves started to change. I watched them steadily increase the more I embodied gratitude. This meant how I felt about being grateful changed my brain waves.

Most of us can't access gamma waves, but by the end of my time at the retreat mine were at peak activity. In other words, getting better at gratitude actually rewired my brain.

As the gamma waves on my brain scan rose, so did my intuition and creativity. Naturally, increasing these skills have benefitted me as a leader in the time that followed, as it would benefit any leader.

My embodied gratitude practice unlocked parts of my brain I had never accessed before. I saw it for myself.

Practical Applications For Leaders

It is one thing to say "be more grateful," but how do you actually make yourself do it?

Even those of us who want to replace performative gestures of gratitude with deeply embodied ones may find it easier said than done. Changing long-held mental and emotional habits is not quite the same as scheduling a block of time to go to the gym each morning or creating a process to check your email at set periods twice a day.

In the Buddhist practice of self-reflection called Naikan, practitioners are encouraged to regularly use prompts to look inward at various areas in one's own life, from work to friendships to social action to relationships. Gratitude researcher Robert Emmons, who we encountered earlier, adapted this process in his own work to lay out three questions that he suggests people ask themselves and reflect on for ten minutes each day.

The first question is: "What support, kindness, or care have I received from others?" The second is: "What have I shared or contributed to others?" And, the third is: "What difficulty or trouble have I been the cause of?"

The trick is to stay consistent with this practice. Building new neural pathways doesn't happen overnight. Like learning to play an instrument, you are trying to map the neurons within your skull to the patterns of how you interact with the world.

Emmons also suggests that it is important to build moments of stillness into your day (sound familiar?). What he specifically recommends is to layer on top of pure stillness a specific focus on gratitude.

The idea here is to associate the negative emotion of stress with the positive, enriching sensation of gratitude. More brain wiring. Just like when you are looking into the eyes of your pet or a loved one, the feeling of love is accompanied by the release of oxytocin, the hormone that makes you feel that trust and bond. When you embody gratitude, you feel it in your body. And I'm asking you to give yourself permission to feel good when you offer gratitude.

In short, leaders who truly want to embody gratitude are building a habit, and it is a habit that might be new for many of them. So, start small. Thank a single team member for their contribution.

Give one person a small, heartfelt, concrete token of your thanks. Carve out real time to present this specific token of thanks with an explanation of why you chose it. An inexpensive personal gift attached to what the person loves or what they've done is infinitely more meaningful than a mail-merged holiday card blast or even a mass getaway retreat.

Acts of gratitude may not scale, but their benefits will be exponential and outsized.

A Few Last Words on Your Buddha Nature

At the heart of the insights and teachings of the philosopher named Siddhartha Gautama, or the Buddha, is a simple concept about which many people agonize, but which, when looked at differently, can be incredibly liberating.

It is this:

Nothing is permanent.

Absolutely nothing.

The career you spend so much time pulling out your hair about.

Your home and car and resume.

Your title and salary.

The business you spent hours, weeks, months, and years building with your own hands. The corporation whose rungs you've steadily climbed.

Your family. Your friends. Your spouse or partner. Your children. Your life. The planet Earth. The galaxy. The Universe.

Given enough time, everything we love disappears. But so does everything we hate. The financial issues. The organizational roadblocks. The interpersonal squabbles. The product launch fiascos. The people on your team who won't complete tasks the way you want them completed.

You.

It all goes away.

It is the one thing we all have in common. But if you're reading this, you're here now. You're present in this messy world with all its problems and joys and twists and turns and celebrations and disappointments. One day you won't be here. None of it will be.

But right now you are.

If that's not a reason to be grateful, I don't know what is.

Making It Happen

Stop performing gratitude. The thank you cards given on predetermined holidays, the empty words of appreciation, the tactical maneuvers to try to get people in your good graces. Just cut it out. None of this leads to the benefits you're going for, at least in the short term. And people can see right through it.

When the sensation of gratitude wells up inside you, act on it. Express it. When you act from this place, people will be touched. It goes a long way.

Rewire your brain. Gratitude is formed through your neural pathways just like all other habits, regular behaviors, emotions, and attitudes. Just vowing to be more grateful won't do the trick. You've got to practice.

Ask yourself the three Naikan questions. Do mindful gratitude pauses. Start small. Don't think about scaling your gratitude efforts. That's the kind of smart that's really stupid. Gratitude is a person-by-person affair.

Remember it's all impermanent. Once you realize all the stuff you're taking so deadly seriously won't be there one day, it becomes much easier to become profoundly grateful for what you have in front of you right in the very moment in which you find yourself.

A few guiding questions to help you access your Buddha nature:

1. What are some examples of performative gratitude that you have engaged in, encountered or experienced?

_____

_____

_____

_____

2. What are some concrete ways you could imagine embodying gratitude in the future?

_____

_____

_____

_____

3. Write down one person you are especially grateful for, along with why you are grateful for them. Then list 3-5 actions you can take to express your gratitude that tie in directly with those reasons.

_____

_____

_____

_____

Chapter 3

PRACTICE IMPERMANENCE

Not long ago a friend of mine sent me a video clip he felt I needed to see.

Anderson Cooper was interviewing a pot-bellied man with a wizard beard and a halo of gray hair fringing a nearly bare scalp. The setting was a minimalist white-walled room.

The clip was labeled "Rick Rubin—60 Minutes Interview".

I didn't recognize the name. At first, I assumed he was a spiritual leader of some kind.

Rick Rubin, as I soon found out, is a legendary music producer. He first achieved fame as the sonic mastermind behind many of hip hop's first big albums, including Run DMC's *Raising Hell*, L.L. Cool J's *Radio,* and the Beastie Boys' *License to Ill* (all three of which, by the way, I saw play in St. Louis at the 1988 Raising Hell Tour). He went on to usher into existence mega-hits such as The Red Hot Chili Peppers' *BloodSugarSexMagic*, Slayer's *Reign In Blood*, and Tom Petty's *Wild Flowers*. He also revitalized Johnny Cash's career almost singlehandedly and cofounded Def Jam records.

Rubin lacks the self-congratulatory bombast normally associated with top music industry powerhouses. In fact, during the interview, he quickly volunteered that he can barely play any instruments, read music, or work a soundboard.

Anderson Cooper, apparently amused by this admission, asked him what artists pay him for.

Rubin replied, "I'm decisive about what I like and don't like."

About a third of the way through the interview, Cooper made an observation.

"I've never been in a recording studio where there's no gold records and Grammys," he said. "Do you have a tiny ego room somewhere?"

"I don't," Rubin responded with a mischievous smile. "I used to send them all to my parents. I don't know where they are now."

Cooper laughed, but Rubin wasn't finished. "It's a distraction," he continued. "If you start thinking about doing something to achieve that, then you're not focused on making this beautiful thing. It undermines the purity of the project."

I finally understood why my friend had wanted me to see this clip.

When Joe and I got married, we didn't hire a wedding videographer. A video would have certainly allowed us to look back at who was dancing with whom and what my expression was when Joe sang to me. But even before it happened, I understood that our wedding would be no more than a moment in what I hoped would be a life full of experiences together. And so, I was able to fully immerse myself in the day itself.

Likewise, when I decided it was time to retire from serious concert dance, I choreographed, organized, and prepared for a final professional performance. I threw myself into it in every way. I hired an understudy during rehearsals so I could see, adjust, and perfect every detail of the performance from the outside as well as from within. I worked with a yoga teacher to warm me up so I didn't have to warm myself up. I hired a dresser so that in between each piece so I could sit down, which reduced the lactic acid build up in my quads. I determined exactly what I should eat and when based on how my body processed protein and carbs so I was not digesting during the show, which would waste precious energy.

The resulting performance was intricate. It was ornate. And it was, I dare say, beautiful. Then it was over, and I passed into my next phase.

In Tibet, Buddhist monks famously create meticulous multi-colored mandalas of sand. They work on them for weeks. Then, as soon as they are finished, they immediately wipe them away.

My performance was like one of those mandalas.

There are countless examples like this in my life. By now, this way of being has become a habit. However, I wasn't always this way. I used to experience frustration over shows that did not get produced and movies that did not get made. I would spend a great deal of time in my thoughts on how I would create work that would resonate and leave a legacy. However, the more I fixated on these matters, the more challenging it was to move through the world. The more time I spent ruminating on legacy, the longer it took me to achieve my goals.

So many of us torture ourselves with concerns that are, ultimately, as thin as rice paper. We agonize over whether our work will get recognized, published, produced, and praised. We wonder whether our children will get into the right schools. We lose sleep over whether we win this award or that appointment or this certification or that accolade.

And then, it all goes away. Just like the sand in a mandala.

The businesses we build, the families we raise, the art we create, the friendships we foster, the books we write, the relationships we cultivate—given enough time, every single one of these will disappear.

Even mountains erode into dust.

I changed my orientation toward life through my Buddhist practice, which teaches that the most fundamental truth of existence is that all things are impermanent. There are many other spiritual and worldly paths that lead to the same understanding.

True wisdom comes from coming to terms with—even embracing—this fundamental reality.

One of the deep ironies of human existence is that the worst way to get what you want is to try to make it permanent. Holding, gripping, and wishing things would stay the same inevitably creates the suffering we are trying to avoid.

Not exactly wise, is it?

Want to know a surefire way to mess up a first date? Constantly remind the person across from you how awful all your past dates were and how you need marriage and children to happen as soon as possible.

How about a method for guaranteeing you'll sabotage a deal? Make sure to rail about how much you need the sale so that you can cover payroll for the rest of the year.

Looking for a system to ensure high employee turnover? Demand unending loyalty from your team members for the rest of their careers and to go on the warpath to try to ruin those who dare to leave you.

What makes Rick Rubin such an excellent music producer is that the only thing that matters to him is the moment in the recording session, the present and immediate work, the current interaction. On the other hand, the entertainment business—and business in general—is littered with the corpses of projects made by people obsessed with achieving certainty and immortality.

The Drawbacks of Chinese Democracy

In January of 1987, a group of miscreants walked into Daryl Dragon's Rumbo Recorders studio in Los Angeles and changed the music world forever.

Izzy Stradlin, Duff McKagen, Steven Adler, Saul "Slash" Hudson, and W. Axl Rose came together from various splintered bands of L.A.'s Sunset Strip scene. From the first time they rehearsed together, they knew they had something special. They quickly threw themselves into their new band, fueled by a common mission to revitalize rock and roll and take over the world.

They called it Guns N' Roses. Within months of forming, they had built a fanatical following who lined up to see them at legendary clubs like The Roxy and The Troubadour. Soon after, the record labels came calling.

By the time they began work on their debut album, *Appetite for Destruction*, Guns N' Roses had, over a tireless run of blistering live performances, fully honed their sound. In the recording studio, they did what they had done onstage. They recorded all the basic tracks in two weeks and spent only a month on overdubs and vocals.

No one in the band had overly high hopes regarding how it would sell.

"We thought we'd made a record that might do as well as, say, Motorhead," said Slash during a 1991 interview in *Musician* magazine. "It was totally uncommercial."

Instead, *Appetite for Destruction* became the best-selling debut album of all time. It has since sold 30 million copies and has gone platinum eighteen times over. According to rock and culture writer Chuck Klosterman in his bestselling book *Fargo Rock City*, "*Appetite for Destruction* . . . is the best record of the 1980s, regardless of genre. If asked to list the ten best rock albums, this is the only pop metal release that might make the list."

Fast forward to 1998.

At some point, singer Axl Rose began to see himself as the band's undisputed leader and made no secret of it. His increasing insistence on making all of the decisions without input from the other members drove them away. Freed from the interference of his bandmates, Axl felt empowered by past successes to spend as much time and money as he wanted.

He obsessed over every detail of the production. He hired, fired, hired again, and fired again countless musicians. He cycled through producers, including, for a short time, the electronica artist Moby. Axl and his rotating cast of musicians tracked three-hundred hours of ideas, loops, and snippets—ranging from three seconds to three minutes long—each tagged with an ID and arranged and rearranged in near-infinite combinations.

The recording process stretched on and on, through the end of the 1990s and well into the first years of the 2000s. As Axl witnessed musical tastes and trends transform around him, he backed up and reworked the album to incorporate these new styles. Costs skyrocketed. Second and third generation band members quit in frustration.

By this point, in Axl's mind, this was no mere collection of songs. With so much time and money and creative energy sunk into the album—now entitled *Chinese Democracy*—it had to be the capstone of Axl's lifework; a distillation of everything he knew about music.

Geffen Records gave the Guns N' Roses singer a great deal of leeway in making *Chinese Democracy,* but after almost a decade of delays, they had had enough. The label announced publicly that, after having already sunk $13 million dollars into the production of the album, Axl Rose would be responsible for funding the rest of it to completion.

Meanwhile, in the public eye, *Chinese Democracy* had started to become somewhat of a joke. Pop punk band The Offspring released a prank press release announcing *their* next album would be called *Chinese Democracy (You Snooze, You Lose).*

Axl Rose hit them with a cease-and-desist order.

And then, finally, in 2008, a release date for the album was announced.

The big day arrived.

Chinese Democracy came.

And it went.

I know that in my case I've choreographed to the music from *Appetite for Destruction* many times and even used its opening track "Welcome to the Jungle" as the pre-show music to my "The Art of The Big Talk" masterclass.

I have never once listened to *Chinese Democracy.*

I was not alone. Many fans had moved on to other interests long before and ignored it completely. The ones who bothered to give it a listen tended to find it unremarkable.

Crushed, Axl Rose disappeared from public view for nearly a decade.

The story does have a happy ending, though. In 2016, original members of Guns N' Roses—Duff McKagen, Slash, and . . . yes, Axl Rose . . . announced that they would be reuniting to tour together for the first time in decades. They had apparently repaired their personal relationships and realized what had caused them to enjoy making music together so much in the first place.

Shows sold out within minutes. Original fans brought their children and screamed along with every word. Critics proclaimed that the magic was back, that they sounded better than ever, that musicians half their age were playing only with a quarter of their energy.

The majority of the songs they performed came from *Appetite for Destruction.*

Impermanence and the Meaningful Life

It might seem from some of the examples I've chosen that my point is that you should simply live for the moment, avoid planning, and forget about details.

Not at all.

In a 2017 article called "Why You Should Pretend Today Is the End" written by former marketing wunderkind, bestselling author, and pop philosopher Ryan Holiday for the *New York Observer,* the author calls out the popular trope about how people would spend their time if they knew the world was ending tomorrow.

"It might seem liberating," he writes, "but in truth would be quite terrible. Who would follow the law? Who would care about anyone but themselves? What would get done? At the end of that day, you'd be grateful the world was not ending."

Holiday goes on to make clear the distinction between living life nihilistically, with no thought at all to the future, and living with the awareness of impermanence in your bones. In doing so, he offers the analogy of how soldiers might behave knowing they are about to deploy to a dangerous area of the world.

"They get their affairs in order," he writes. "They handle their business. They tell their children or their family that they love them. They don't have time for quarreling or petty matters. And then in the morning they are ready to go—hoping to come back in one piece but prepared for the possibility that they may not."

We tend to believe that conscientiousness comes from fixating on what we can control. If we could only get better at time blocking or eliminating distractions or creating priority-ranked To-Do lists, we could finally achieve everything we ever wanted to achieve.

It doesn't work that way.

This is not to say that time-management and organizational tactics are not valuable tools. They can be very useful, and I take advantage of them regularly. However, unpaired with a fundamental shift of one's understanding about the true nature of reality, they all become impotent. A successful life—a meaningful life—comes from learning to walk a line between residing fully in the moment and attuning yourself to the ecosystem of time, space, and relationships within which you exist.

"Don't live each day as *if* the world is ending," writes Ryan Holiday. "That would be a disaster. Live your life as if you're not sure whether your time on this earth is ending or not."

In order to constantly remind himself of this reality, Holiday commissioned the creation of two coins, which he carries with him everywhere. One says Memento Mori on it, which means "remember you will die" in Latin. The other says Amor Fati, which means "the love of fate."

He looks at these coins every day—multiple times per day—both because he understands how easy it is to forget their lessons and to practice living each step of his life in accordance with them.

Understanding impermanence is important. However, it is only by practice that you gain the tools to live your life in a fully engaged way.

The Impermanence Practice

Canadian experimental psychologist Donald Hebb spent the early part of his career studying the function of neurons in learning. In 1949, he published his findings in a book called *The Organization of Behavior* that would completely revolutionize our modern understanding of intelligence, behavior, and habit formation.

Hebb's central premise was that when loosely connected behaviors are regularly repeated over an extended period of time, the brain makes corresponding physical connections.

"When an axon of cell A is near enough to excite cell B and repeatedly or persistently takes part in firing it," he wrote, "some growth process or metabolic changes takes place in one or both cells such that A's efficiency, as one of the cells. Firing B, is increased."

Plain English: "Neurons that fire together wire together."

In short, our brains initially take in each segment of whatever we're trying to learn as a bunch of discrete steps, with separate neurons dedicated to each. The more you practice them in conjunction, the more intertwined these nerve cells become.

For example, when a dancer first learns how to execute a plié, the most fundamental and crucial dance step, they are extremely conscious of all the separate parts of the movement. The bend at the knees. The turnout of the feet. The positioning of the hips and torso. The carrying of the arms. What makes it awkward and uncomfortable at this stage is that the brain still has to dedicate distinct neurons to each individual movement.

However, as the dancer repeats these movements in conjunction over and over again, the neurons dedicated to each of the parts "fire together." Soon, as Hebb observed, they begin to "wire together." Now the dancer's brain—and, by extension, body—performs the action as one coordinated whole. It happens seamlessly, almost without thought. It becomes as easy as walking.

In fact, it is by exactly this process that we do learn to walk. It is how we learn to drive a car, throw baseballs, shoot hoops, tie our shoes, knot a tie, and brush our teeth.

It is also the process by which we learn emotional habits. How we learn to run from relationships the moment someone brings up commitment. How we learn to react with rage at innocuous comments. How we learn to respond to a loved one with warmth when they smile at us or hug our children when they skin their knees.

Repetition of the simplest and most profound positive mental habits is what causes them to stick, because . . . what fires together wires together.

Whether he knows it or not, Ryan Holiday is using this sort of repetitive association to reinforce his ability to approach the challenges of his life through the lens of impermanence. His track record of executing a wide range of successful projects, amassing a following of admiring fans, while maintaining strong relationships with family and friends takes roots in this practice and others like it.

Your preferred method of practicing impermanence may vary widely from Holiday's. The specifics will depend on the dynamics of your own life and career. But whatever practice you choose, it must be regular and it must be consistent. Otherwise, whatever knowledge you glean will be purely theoretical.

What follows are some ideas drawn from my own practice. I invite you to use them as a starting point.

Tracking Emotional States

As human beings, we often see ourselves as the "rational species," but we are overwhelmingly driven by our emotions.

Over the course of any given day, we might go from happy to sad, content to annoyed, calm to angry. And, whenever we experience one of these emotional states, it feels completely real. It seems to us we will always feel this way.

There is a concept in certain schools of Buddhism known as the Ten Worlds. The idea is that we each have states within ourselves that get reflected into the outside world as we pass through them. All of us have the potential to experience any of these states at any time and shift between them rapidly. They range from Hell (suffering, feeling of powerlessness) to Animality (ruled by instinct) to Heaven (intense pleasure from satiating a desire) to Buddhahood (transcendent freedom).

We don't move through these states from lowest to highest and stay there. We bounce back and forth between them for reasons of which we are barely aware.

How do we keep our actions from pinballing along with our states?

One way is to track them as they are occurring.

Whenever you are experiencing a certain state, mark it down in a notebook, in your computer, or in the Notes app on your phone. Tag it with a time and a date. Specifically acknowledge what you are experiencing in the moment—whether it is agitation, frustration, wishing, wanting, or joy.

After about a month, look back on what you've tracked. Did you notice any patterns? How often did your state change? Did it ever feel overwhelming only to disappear from your memory a day or two later?

What you'll probably find is that your emotional states shift like the sands of a mandala. Undertaking this exercise will train you to deal with the raw material of your emotions as they really are—impermanent.

The "What Happens If?" Exercise

We are all mental time-travelers.

When we come across a potential new client, we immediately go to "What will happen if I can't close the deal?" Or we think, "Imagine all the things I'll be able to buy."

When we hear an unsteady word from an existing client, our minds skip ahead to potential catastrophe.

If a star employee calls in sick, we imagine them taking a job interview, along with the inevitable disaster that will accompany their departure.

Often, we deal with our rapid-fire brains by pushing these thoughts away. We pretend—if only to ourselves—that the worst-case scenarios will never happen. Our clients will never move to another vendor. Our best employees will always stay with us. We will always work at the same place.

In other words, we simultaneously cling onto exactly how things are while failing to prepare for inevitable reversals.

What if, instead, we faced our "what-ifs" head on? What if we dug into them and took them to their logical conclusions?

So . . . let's say your "what if" is about the potential of losing your biggest client.

Take yourself through the following internal dialogue.

What if I lose my biggest client?

I'll have less revenue next year.

What if I have less revenue next year?

I won't be able to give myself a raise.

What if I can't give myself a raise?

I won't be able to go to as many fancy dinners.

What if I can't go to as many fancy dinners?

I'll be disappointed and annoyed.

What if you're disappointed and annoyed?

See what I did there.

When you take back control of the "what if" game in this way, you'll find that the worst-case scenario is usually survivable.

Examine Your Stories and Your Lies

Fighting the reality of impermanence keeps us constructing and believing our own stories and lies.

A "story" is a projection of the future.

For example: *When I sell my business, I'll have the most amazing life ever.*

A lie is a contingent belief you have about yourself.

If I take off a weekend on the road to selling my business, I'm a lazy person.

Our brains construct both stories and lies on an automatic basis. By dissecting them, they lose their power.

Because when you tell yourself your life will be one way when a certain situation happens, you are behaving as if your story has an ending. An ending implies permanence. You may get some of what you want—for a certain stretch of time—when you sell your business. But life will go on. New challenges will come up. The shifting sands of reality means you have no way of knowing what the outcome will be and how long it will last.

The same goes for the lies you tell yourself. In the example I've used, besides the obvious reality that everyone needs rest, believing in some immutable characteristic you have *(I'm lazy)* is a fallacy based on a rigid view of life. It is concrete, rather than sand.

The antidote to stories and lies is to collect evidence.

Can you think of an example where you achieved a goal and your problems didn't all disappear?

Can you come up with any examples when you worked really hard? Do you display lazy tendencies in each and every instance?

It's incredibly liberating. And this kind of freedom is wise.

Keep Connecting with Your Gratitude

Every single time I have a meeting with my team, I schedule a few minutes for myself to sit in stillness beforehand and reflect on how grateful I am for them. My ability to confidently carve out this time no matter how much else I have going on comes from my understanding of how this next meeting could conceivably be the last time we have together. Similarly, I make sure I carve out time every week to let all of my team members know how much they mean to me.

Twice a month, I remind myself that everybody I work with—from my team members to my clients—will one day leave me (whether in six months or twenty-five years). Reciting this truism to myself allows me to embrace it when it eventually comes.

Before I have a conversation with anyone, I set my intentions first. I literally write them down. Even if the conversation goes in a different direction than I expected, I'll know I have practiced giving the interaction the seriousness of purpose with which all temporary things deserve. And all things are temporary.

Each quarter, I schedule a meeting with myself to work on building additional redundancy into my business. Even the best team members, products, services, and systems, are ... you guessed it ... impermanent. By forcing myself to periodically focus on the worst-case scenario—a key team member ends his engagement with us unexpectedly, we lose our biggest client, a new technology makes my business model obsolete—I generate alternatives.

Again, these are simply methods that work for me. Yours will probably be different. But whatever you choose, establishing a practice of encoding into your brain, your heart, and your soul the beautiful and terrible reality of how it all goes away, will free you to turn your life into your own personal platinum record.

Making It Happen

Put the mementos of past victories in your basement. Or your storage unit, if you're a New Yorker like me. If you can't bear to do this literally, train yourself to ignore them as much as possible. Although it can be helpful to take some measure of confidence from past wins, they are ultimately dead and gone. Learn to focus on the project, challenge, and people in front of you.

Stop obsessing over what you're working on as if it's the only project you'll ever undertake. If you view every engagement, business, and initiative as one of many, it will liberate you to do even better work than you would have otherwise.

Create rituals of repetition. It is not enough to understand impermanence; you must practice it. Remember, what fires together wires together.

Track your emotional states, ask what if your "what-ifs" happen, examine your stories and your lies.

Build time into your schedule to get still, set intention, and dive into your gratitude. We've covered some of these ideas already, but when you come to them with the fundamental knowledge of impermanence, they take on a whole new level of significance.

A few guiding questions to help you access your Buddha nature:

1. What would you do differently if you honestly faced the fact that you have no idea of whether or not you'll really be around tomorrow?

_____

_____

_____

_____

2. Play a round of the "what if" game with the issue in your life that is troubling you most . . .

*What if?*_____

_____

*What if?*_____

_____

*What if?*_____

_____

3. Brainstorm ways you can reduce the weight you place on any one of your products or initiatives.

_____

_____

_____

_____

Chapter 4

LET GO

I have loved the movie *Swingers* ever since it came out in 1997.

If you haven't seen it, please put down this book and rent or stream it immediately. It's the story of a bunch of aspiring twenty-something actors navigating their dating lives at the swing dancing clubs that briefly became a craze in late-Nineties Los Angeles. The movie launched the careers of future stars Vince Vaughan, Heather Graham, Jon Favreau, and Ron Livingston.

It has amazing dance sequences (which, of course, gives it even extra appeal to me). It is stuffed full of hilarious one-liners. It is a modern comedy classic.

It is also a deeply Buddhist film.

Above all, the movie is about the importance—and power—of letting go.

When we meet the protagonist, Mikey, he is living in L.A. and wallowing in misery because his long-term girlfriend from back home broke up with him six months earlier. His friends are constantly taking him out to clubs and lounges trying to get him to have fun and move on. His hyper-fixation on the past, on his own needs, and on the perceptions of others continually derail his efforts.

My own favorite scene reveals this confluence of self-sabotage perfectly.

Let me paint the picture for you.

Mikey gets home from a night on the town. He has just met a lovely young woman named Nikki and got her number. Instead of falling asleep happy, he paces in his undershirt.

Finally, he picks up the phone and calls Nikki.

Remember, this is still the late twentieth century, so we are in the age of the answering machine. The series of messages he proceeds to leave on hers will ensure this film's enshrinement in the annals of comedy for eons to come.

Mikey's first message: "Hi, uh, this is Mike. I met you at the, um, Dresden tonight. I just called to say that I had a great time . . . and you should call me tomorrow, or in two days, whatever. Anyway, my number is 213-555-4679—"

The machine beeps and cuts him off (which, for those of you born too late to have experienced it, is what would happen when you went on for too long).

He immediately calls her back again.

Mikey's second message: "Hi, Nikki, this is Mike again. I just called cause it sounded like your machine might've cut me off when I, before I finished leaving my number. Anyway, uh, and, you know, and also, sorry to call so late, but you were still at the Dresden when I left so I knew I'd get your machine. Anyhow, my number's 21—"

Another beep. Cut off again.

Now he's clenching the phone. Grimacing.

He punches in Nikki's number for the third time.

"213-555-4679. That's it. I just wanna leave my number. I didn't want you to think I was weird or desperate or ... we should just hang out and see where it goes cause it's nice and, you know, no expectations. Okay. Thanks a lot. Bye bye."

He walks away from the phone. Within seconds, he rushes back over to it.

He calls her back.

The answering machine picks up.

"I just got out of a six-year relationship, okay," Mikey says. "That should help explain why I'm acting so weird. I just wanted you to know that. It's not you, it's me. I'm sorry."

In a small, already-beaten voice, he adds, "This is Mike."

The painful episode is still not finished, though.

He picks up the phone again.

"Hi Nikki, this is Mike. Could you just call me when you get in? I'm gonna be up for a while and I'd just rather speak to you in person instead of trying to fit it all into—"

Beep.

He is beside himself.

He curses loudly.

And ...

He calls back again.

"Uh, Nikki?" he says. "Mike. It's uh, uh, it's just, uh, this just isn't working out. I think you're great, but maybe we should take some time off from each other. It's not you, it's me. It's what I'm going through, alright? It's uh ... it's only been six months ..."

Someone picks up on the other end of the line.

It's Nikki.

"Mike?"

"Nikki? Great! Did you just walk in or were you listening all along?"

"Don't ever call me again."

It's hard to watch, but we've all been there.

Mikey, like so many of us, is trapped in a cycle of suffering.

He is full of assumptions based on everything but actual reality. He is creating a web of possible futures based only on his own imagination. His preexisting beliefs are causing him to sabotage that which he wants most before he even truly gets started.

To release himself from this cycle of suffering, Mikey will have to learn how to *let go*.

So will we.

Letting Go of Assumptions

Assumptions are entrenched opinions we form about situations, people, or outcomes without concrete evidence. They often stem from fears, insecurities, and, above all, past experiences.

They act as invisible baggage, weighing us down emotionally and distorting our perspective.

The story of how the upstart Netflix annihilated the corporate behemoth Blockbuster has become legend. According to the "official" version, the Netflix founders approached Blockbuster in the early stages of the company and presented them with an idea for the two companies to work together to integrate the brick-and-mortar and offline services into one entity.

Reed Hastings, the Netflix founder who made the proposal, was dismissed and, in the words of business journalist Greg Satell, "laughed out of the room."

A decade after this fateful meeting, Blockbuster was driven into bankruptcy, in no small part due to the ubiquity of Netflix. Since then, Netflix has become one of the most valuable companies in the world.

The details of what really happened are, as usual, more interesting.

For one, the reputation of Blockbuster CEO John Antioco as a blunderer completely lacking foresight is largely undeserved. He understood the business model of the company he led inside and out. He knew that a huge portion of their revenue came from customer late fees. Profitability depended on them.

Although late fees were an annoyance to customers, they were simply part of how the rental video industry worked. They were baked into its fabric.

In other words, John Antioco was attached to his assumptions about his business.

With the benefit of hindsight, it is tempting to scorn Antioco for clinging to such outmoded assumptions. But try to place yourself in his shoes for a moment. It had always been an article of faith that without late fees, customers would have no reason to ever return the videos they borrowed. What had started as a practical solution to a real problem had, even in the face of new technology, become an end in and of itself.

Antioco's attachment to industry assumptions certainly kept him from broadening his gaze to identify counterintuitive solutions that would have better served his business, but he was far from alone in this. Also, believe it or not, he was one of the first to attempt to adjust.

When the CEO recognized the threat Netflix posed, he discontinued late fees and launched Blockbuster Online. It's hard to remember this now, but when Blockbuster Online came out, it was popular. It allowed members to order DVDs on the web and pick up or return videos at a nearby store.

Quite a few Netflix customers switched over at the time.

Antioco gets a lot of flak for his decision not to acquire Netflix. However, Netflix was not yet dominant when he launched the new hybrid model. It is not hard to imagine a scenario where his shift turned the ship around and maintained Blockbuster's dominance.

While perhaps later than would have been ideal, John Antioco was able to challenge his own assumptions.

Unfortunately, other powerful stakeholders in the company were not.

Because it was such a major change, the short-term result would have been a $400 million shortfall in yearly revenue. This number, while certainly large in absolute terms, was a manageable amount for a company Blockbuster's size. However, fellow executive Jim Keyes put together an analysis of the costs of Antioco's changes and circulated it among key personnel. One of the recipients of this analysis was Carl Ichan, a powerful and active investor in the company.

Icahn lobbied the board to oust Antioco. He succeeded.

Keyes became CEO.

He reinstated late fees. He nixed Blockbuster Online.

The company was bankrupt within five years.

Today it no longer exists.

There's an old joke where two fish are swimming along and one says to the other, "How's the water?"

The second one looks at the first and replies: "What's water?"

Assumptions are like the water we swim in.

Typically, we barely notice them because they form the environment in which we operate. This environment is constructed, but it's constructed of really strong stuff. Our upbringing. Our culture. Our training. Our past experiences.

These assumptions can help us swim through our day to day. But sometimes, when unusual challenges arise or the real environment changes, they no longer apply and we have to let them go.

The certainty that the video rental business depends on late fees was the water the Blockbuster executives swam in.

They ended up drowning.

Letting Go of Imagined Futures

"When my business makes its first million, I will finally be able to relax."

"When I get that raise, everything will fall into place."

"When I get married, I'll have the most amazing life ever."

The human imagination is a truly powerful force. So often, the imagined scenarios we create about the future shape our expectations and emotional attachments even more intensely than the concrete reality right in front of us.

Nature (or evolution or God or the divine spirit) programmed us to construct and feel the power of this psychological time traveling because it is incredibly motivating. This doesn't mean it is accurate.

Bud Tribble, an early Apple employee borrowed a term from a Star Trek episode in which aliens used their minds to create a mass hallucination for the crew of the starship *Enterprise* to describe the modus operandi of his boss Steve Jobs.

He called it the "reality distortion field".

Jobs had an uncanny ability to get Apple designers and developers to fanatically dedicate themselves—often sacrificing every other aspect of their lives—to achieving whatever agenda he persuaded them was essential to their own wellbeing and fulfillment, as well as that of humanity as a whole.

Attached to this bold vision was the implication that there was an end point to the unceasing urgency, frantic berating, and back-breaking hours that characterized life at Apple.

There was not.

Steve Jobs was certainly smart. Through imagination, force of will, and reality manipulation, he was able to recraft the world in his own image. And he got what he wanted out of his employees in the service of that image.

But was he wise?

I remember a time when I would ride the New York City subway and almost every commuter was reading a book. Today books have all but vanished there. Instead, almost every person riding the subway is hunched, glassy-eyed, over their iPhones scrolling through thirty-second videos clips.

It has become a virtual consensus among psychologists, and child development experts, that smartphones have precipitated a mental health crisis among young people the likes of which society hasn't seen for generations. In fact, a recent Surgeon General warning places iPhones and their descendants on par with health-wrecking products like cigarettes.

Disconnection between family members is at an all-time high. People slam into each other in the streets because they are looking at their phone screens instead of paying attention to their surroundings. "Screen addiction" treatment centers are springing up throughout the country.

Entrepreneur Elizabeth Holmes was obsessed with Steve Jobs. She adopted his signature black turtlenecks as her own and lowered her voice to sound more like someone of his ilk.

She also adopted the reality distortion field in a big way.

Her company Theranos was based on the development and production of a medical device she claimed would be able read all of your vitals with one pinprick of blood. I can only assume she initially thought the idea would work. But whether it worked or not didn't seem to be her major concern.

What appears to have been behind her every move was an unabating hunger and attachment to the idea that becoming a legendary startup founder was not only inevitable but integral to her own happiness and fulfillment.

It was almost certainly this grasping onto her imagined future that caused her to pretend the product still worked even when it was clear it didn't. It was what caused her to continue to raise money and tout the benefits to humanity for a product she rationally knew delivered no value and which actually could cause serious harm.

Her sense of self-worth was so thoroughly tied to her desired future that she reality-distorted herself right into prison.

This is not to say that there are no benefits to Apple products or tech startups. Or that it doesn't make sense to envision a better future or dream big. It's not a screed against discipline or hard work or going after what you want.

My point is only that the narratives we construct about ourselves, where we need to go, the certainty we often have about what will be meaningful and happy-making in the future and what we need to do to get there are just that . . . narratives.

Fictions.

There is no way of knowing whether what we are so hungry to achieve will make us feel the way we want to feel or even lead to the outcomes we want to bring about.

Wise leadership requires letting go of any one future and detaching your ego from what you imagine that future will bring you. Not only does the alternative cause serious issues for yourself and those around you; it is usually wrong.

Letting Go of Beliefs

"If I take Saturday and Sunday off, I'm a lazy person and will never be a success."

"If I don't berate my employees, I'm a pushover."

"If I forgive that person, I'm weak."

"If I draw a firm boundary, I'm unreasonable and mean."

Assumptions are other-focused. They are about how people will perceive us or how the structures, systems, and institutions we move within operate. Imagined futures are time-related. They are about our certainties about where we need to end up.

Beliefs are about ourselves.

And they all too often veer toward the negative.

A lot of times, these beliefs about ourselves have deep roots—lessons we pick up from our parents and the cultures in which we are reared. Even when they are inaccurate, they can feel as real as the ground we stand on.

Remember, what fires together wires together.

We must use every method at our disposal to sift lies from truth and erode the power that the former have over us. Holding onto lies, especially those we tell ourselves, leads to self-judgment and reactive decision making. Plus, since these lies are wired into you, simply seeking to ameliorate them by chasing that which is outside of you may give you relief for a time, but it will inevitably be temporary.

And the aftermath will be even more painful than what preceded it. As I write this book, I'm attached to direct a Broadway musical called *Behind The Curtain*, written by Joe Ricci (yes, my husband Joe), about the life of Johnny Carson.

Johnny Carson was beloved as no talk show host before or after him. Millions of Americans curled up with him before bed each night, charmed and comforted by his public warmth and familiarity. Every late-night talk show host since him—from Jay Leno to David Letterman to Jimmy Fallon—has held him up as the gold standard to which to aspire.

His guests adored him as well. The most powerful members of the Hollywood elite clamored to get a coveted spot on his show. He was inclusive of all different kinds of people before it was the norm.

This public persona was the exact opposite of how he was when the camera lights went off.

Carson grew up with a cold, domineering, and approval-withholding mother. He scrapped and clawed and climbed to prove himself worthy of her.

He reached the pinnacle of his field. But when it came to his mother, it had no effect. She was unmoved by his achievements. She made it clear she thought his show was foolish. Until her death, she regularly expressed to him that he was wasting his time. As such, his accomplishments were never able to fill the hole at the center of his soul.

Unable to ameliorate his deepest beliefs about himself with worldly success, he became sullen and solitary. He was unable to sustain any relationship. He became cruel to the people closest to him.

I fell for him, just like the rest of America. What I discovered through my research about the shadow side of this American icon has never left me. In many ways, it has served as a cautionary tale.

The tragedy of Johnny Carson was that despite his army of admirers, he ultimately died alone.

It is all-too-human to try to cover up or run away from the beliefs we have about ourselves, whether it is by chasing external validation and markers of success. But running away and covering up are not the same as letting go.

The level of intensity with which these issues face us vary widely. Even when we feel we have our lives in order, our beliefs often run in the background making us less effective than we could be otherwise.

It is one thing to say we should let go of our false beliefs—and our assumptions and our imagined futures—but it is another to develop an understanding of how to do so. What follows are a few tactics to help get you there.

Build a Case

The question remains: How can we tell if our assumptions are misguided? Or if our futures really are imaginary? Or whether our beliefs are false?

Some would say we should just talk positively to ourselves or act as-if.

The problem with this approach is that the moment we see something out in the world that contradicts our new unfounded narrative, it all falls apart.

Neural wiring is very strong.

The antidote?

Build a case for yourself.

For example, let's say you take off two days in a row and translate that into a belief that you are a fundamentally lazy person.

Instead of using this mental flash as an excuse to beat yourself up—or simply shutting it down—get curious. Examine it. Ask yourself why you feel this way. And then, like a detective investigating a hunch or a scientist seeking to test the validity of a hypothesis—begin to test it.

Do you always do the bare minimum amount of work? Every single time? Are there times where you work when other people don't? Have you developed systems to become more efficient than other people so you don't have to work every Sunday?

And don't just run this through as a momentary exercise in your mind. Really track it. Observe the hypothesis for the next week or two and write down confirming or disconfirming data. Build a case one way or another. And do so without judgment, but rather, with curiosity.

Curiosity encourages a mindset of exploration rather than judgment, helping us question the validity of our thoughts and uncover deeper truths. By asking open-ended questions like, "Is this true, or is this a lie I'm telling myself?" or "What am I basing this on?" we can challenge the foundations of our narratives.

Curiosity also helps align us with our authentic selves by prompting deeper reflection, such as, "What is true about me?" or "What is my core?" Through curiosity, we replace rigid, limiting beliefs with constructive perspectives that empower growth and adaptability.

What you'll usually find is that your presumption is false. But even if there is some truth to it, you'll be armed with the information you need to dispassionately put yourself on the path to change.

As such, you'll be able to let it go.

We tend to obsess over our characteristics, especially in relation to what is happening to us (and because of us).

Your characteristics, which include traits, but also roles, titles, and achievements almost invariably change over time and according to circumstance. However, underneath all of these characteristics, there is character—your truest self.

Ask yourself what people have said about you for as long as you can remember. I'm talking about higher-level aspects of yourself like kindness, integrity, or perseverance. The unwavering truth about who you are. When you lock in on this, when you gain clarity about your essence, you will be able to far more readily let go of superficial identities and false beliefs. It will become increasingly easier to align your actions and decisions with your fundamental character.

Or, as certain wise leaders would call it . . . your Buddha nature.

Wrapping It Up

The three areas you cling to that hold you (and almost all of us) back are assumptions, imagined futures, and beliefs.

Learn to see the water you swim in even if you're a fish.

Decouple your self-image from the beliefs you have about yourself.

Replace judgment with curiosity.

Rewire your brain curiosity and testing, with evidence collection.

Focus on character, not characteristics.

A few guiding questions to help you access your Buddha nature:

1. What is one imagined future that troubles you but which you have no evidence will occur? Write about it here in detail.

2. Write down some assumptions you've been making about the same issue.

3. List some inaccurate beliefs about yourself or your life that have led you down a less-than-ideal path in the past.

Chapter 5

DISCERN

Maria Konnikova was a success by almost every measure.

She and her family emigrated from the Soviet Union just before it collapsed. Despite having known no English before starting school in her new hometown of Acton, Massachusetts, she graduated high school as one of the top students in her class and was accepted by Harvard University. While at Harvard, she double majored in psychology and creative writing and caught the attention of Steven Pinker—an internationally renowned cognitive psychologist and bestselling author–who became her mentor.

At Columbia University, where she enrolled to obtain her PhD in psychology, she was taken under the wing of Walter Mischel, the twenty-fifth most cited psychologist of the twentieth century. Together they conducted research where they observed and quantified the degree to which subjects experienced the perception of agency over their own lives.

From there she became a producer for the *Charlie Rose Show*, launching the program's recurring "Brain Series" segment. In her free time, she wrote articles for *Scientific American*, the *New Yorker*, and the popular *Big Think* blog.

Soon she had an idea for her first book, and she dug in with her customary gusto and focus. The result was *How to Think Like Sherlock Holmes*, which was a major hit. Her follow up, *The Confidence Game*, did even better, earning her a spot on the coveted *New York Times* Bestseller List.

With a track record like hers, it stood to reason that Maria Konnikova felt very much in-control of her destiny.

And then her life completely changed.

"A few years ago, I hit a really hard patch in my life," Konnikova explained to Katherine Milkmen in an interview for the *Knowledge at Wharton* newsletter, "I got really sick, my grandmother died, my husband lost his job, my mom lost her job. It made me stop and think about luck again in a new light, and think about, 'You know what? I've studied the illusion of control. I thought I knew all about it, but it ends up that I probably have some of these illusions myself, because this really caught me off guard.'"

Marika Konnikova responded by doing what she did best.

Research.

She began with a book called *The Theory of Games* by John von Neumann.

Born in 1903, John von Neumann would, during the five-plus decades of his life, transform almost every aspect of human civilization. As part of the Manhattan Project, he was pivotal to the development of the atomic bomb. His improvements to the first electronic computer paved the way for the digital revolution. A mathematical framework he devised made every subsequent development in quantum mechanics possible.

And he created the field of *game theory*.

Von Neumann was a big fan of toys and games well into adulthood. Of all these, there was one that captured his attention more than any other.

Poker.

John von Neumann loved the game of poker. Unlike many of his colleagues, he much preferred it to chess. As he saw it, chess is too perfect. In chess, both players have a full view of what their opponents are doing. There are no external random circumstances that can derail your game.

Poker, on the other hand, is "a game of incomplete information." Players are dealt random cards and have to make do with what they get. Still, unlike roulette or blackjack, certain people consistently excel at poker—some making their living exclusively by playing the game.

As Konnikova explains, "it's not just a game of math . . . it's also a game of humans, and it's a game of intention . . . And that's what fascinated [Von Neumann]. He said, 'If I can solve this, I can basically solve life.'"

Before then, Konnikova had always attacked problems by throwing her sheer force of will at them. Study. Attain advanced degrees. Work hard. Persist. The same kind of grit dancers have.

Misfortune taught her that no matter how much you try to control your circumstances, the chaos of reality will—sooner or later—throw elements at you that you can't do anything about.

She was looking for a new framework for living a good life in the face of this new understanding.

In other words, she wanted to learn how to make wise decisions no matter what cards she was dealt. To do so, she embarked on a side career as a professional poker player.

She became an international champion.

Her journey is documented in her 2020 book *The Biggest Bluff: How I Learned to Pay Attention, Master Myself, and Win*.

Siddhartha Gautama wasn't much of a poker player (maybe because cards hadn't been invented yet), but he spent much of his life wrestling with the same central problem as Maria Konnikova and John von Neumann.

As a young prince, Siddhartha was unable to comprehend the existence of illness, poverty, and hunger. Before he encountered them for the first time, his father had tried to create an illusory world for him free of all these ills. But when he finally did see suffering, he could hardly bear it.

Much of the book you've been reading deals with how this young man—later called the Buddha by his followers—created a set of tools for dealing with the existence of outcomes we can't control despite our best efforts . . . and about how even those of us without a spiritual bent can use these tools to transform our leadership capabilities.

Much like the best poker players, what the Buddha came to understand—and subsequently taught—was that even when you can't control what events happen to you and how other people behave, you can control how you respond to them. In so doing, you can, more times than not, make choices that embody and project wisdom.

This is called discernment.

It is essential for every effective leader to master.

Here's how.

The Consequences of All Actions

Discerning people understand that actions have consequences.

Of course, on a surface level we all know this. We get that if we speed and a cop catches us, we're going to get a ticket. We realize that if we eat a big meal and drink a bottle of cabernet right before going to bed, we are not going to sleep well. Yet, in the day-to-day of how we move throughout the world, so much of what we do is completely divorced from any consideration of consequences.

We tend to do what we do just because . . . well, that's what we do.

Sometimes we engage in a certain behavior based entirely on emotion—driven by how we feel in the moment, regardless of how we might justify that behavior to ourselves and others later. Other times we engage in behaviors purely out of habit.

Or else we might ask advice about what to do from the closest person on hand and run to act on it immediately, never really stopping to consider whether the friend or family member in question has any background that would give them special insight into the situation or whether they are filtering it through their own experiences and attachments.

It would be as if a poker player decided to bet or fold simply based on how they felt in any given moment . . . or because they always bet or fold at 2:00 . . . or because they asked the person next to them whether they should bet or fold.

Whatever cards you get, any move you make will generate a consequence. If you bluff, there will be a consequence. If you double down, there will be a consequence. If you walk away from the table, there will be a consequence.

None of these consequences are necessarily "good" or "bad" in and of themselves. There is no way to completely predict what the results of your actions will be.

You might press your luck on a great hand and get beaten anyway. You might walk away from the table only to see the person who got the cards you would have gotten win the whole pot.

You might fire an underperforming account executive, only to lose a client who—without your knowledge—stayed with you because they liked working with that person. You might invest in a company with a stellar reputation to later find out that one of their executives committed financial malfeasance.

A recognition of consequences is not the same as assigning blame. The point is simply to begin with the understanding that in an uncertain world with incomplete information, there are no perfect decisions. Every action you take will ricochet into a potentially infinite number of results that you might not—often could not—have anticipated. Every action you take will require trade-offs.

This is good news. It keeps you flexible and ready to adjust. By coming from this starting place, you become prepared for whatever might happen next.

Observing Your Thoughts and Abandoning One-Size-Fits-All Solutions

After my wedding, I sobbed uncontrollably for two days straight.

I love Joe. He is smart, kind, supportive, hilarious, and talented. When I met him, I was dating someone else. My heart quickly understood that not only did I no longer want to continue dating the person I was seeing, but also that I never wanted anyone other than Joe again for as long as I lived.

Still, I had also never seen myself as someone who would get married. The *not married* me had long been part of my identity. I didn't need to be married. I had my own career, my own money, my wonderful friends, my ability to date whomever and whenever. And I never wanted children, so being married didn't add to my already amazing life.

So when I decided I wanted to get married to Joe, what happened next surprised me. For example, the book I took on my honeymoon to read by the pool was *Committed* by Elizabeth Gilbert.

Elizabeth Gilbert first became famous for her book *Eat, Pray, Love*, which documented the story of how she left her husband because she wasn't fulfilled and then traveled around the world eating exotic foods, dabbling in exotic religious practices, and having exotic affairs.

The last of these affairs—a hot and heavy fling—ended up turning into something longer term.

This is where *Committed* picks up. It is the story of how her romance with the hot Brazilian recounted in her first blockbuster became something deeper. It talks about her process of deciding whether to marry him.

Much of the book consists of her agonizing over the choice, mainly because she doesn't want to give up her freewheeling lifestyle for domestic boredom. Ultimately, the United States immigration service helps make the decision for her. When it becomes clear that her man would be deported if she doesn't marry him, she does the deed.

The subtext here was that Gilbert was not the marrying type— at least not anymore. Her first marriage was a shackle around her leg as any conventional marriage would have been for a woman of her ambition and free-mindedness. Even her second marriage was essentially a clerical maneuver designed to placate the state while maintaining her de facto independence.

So, yeah, *this* was the book I brought on my honeymoon.

This book was a symbol of the world I was a part of and aspired to. Successful. Artistic. Business-minded. *Smart.*

And all of her writing conveyed the message that marriage was a nuisance and obligation at its best, a torturous imprisonment at its worst.

I see myself as a relatively enlightened person. However, in reflecting back, I now recognize the extent to which the feelings and thoughts I had about marriage were not my own. Even in bringing *Committed* to my honeymoon, I had no conscious awareness that I was feeding my mind with more prefabricated prescriptions about "the way things are" and "what things mean."

That was before I actually took the time to proactively observe my thoughts. Before that, I was still in reactive mode. I was unable to discern.

And so, I made a serious shift. I set aside a large chunk of time, made sure all my companies and commitments were handled and I thought.

Just thought.

And what did I think about?

I thought about my thoughts.

Thinking about thoughts is, in many ways, that which most makes us human. Other animals love, hate, fight, and care for their young. Other animals use tools. Scientists are beginning to recognize that some other animals even have language (dolphins) and use humor (chimps).

But as far as we know, we human beings are the only animal on earth that can conceptualize our own thoughts. We can listen to the largely automatic firings of our brains and say to ourselves "Why did I think that? Where did that thought come from? What does that thought mean? Is that thought accurate?"

I engaged in exactly this exercise.

I labeled the various parts of my thoughts. I sat with them.

Eventually, I also dug deep to attempt to notice whether there was something I had missed, something I had overlooked, perhaps a lie I had told myself which caused me to dive into a marriage with someone I never should have married.

I found none of this.

What I did find when I sifted through the chatter and connected with my intuition was that I was adhering to one-size-fits-all solutions—messages from my environment, from the media I consumed, from "smart" self-help gurus like Elizabeth Gilbert, and from modern myths that one could be a married woman or a free woman but not both.

I had not been discerning between what was right for me and what was filling the air around me.

By thinking about my thoughts I could now do just that.

At the time of writing this book, I have been happily married to Joe for sixteen years.

It was one of the best decisions of my life.

One of the best *discernments* of my life.

Whether you are wrestling with a major decision like who to marry or simply trying to figure out the best time to have a difficult conversation with an employee, build the habit of first setting aside time to think about your thoughts.

Once you've acknowledged what's going on in that brain of yours, you next need to figure out what it all means. And this process doesn't have to be an intellectual one. Like all of us, you bring outside baggage to the table but you also have a finely-honed intuition.

What you'll find when you build a practice of thinking about your thoughts is that just because your colleagues, culture, family, friends, and even your self-image say you should apply X solution to Y problem, that doesn't mean it's the right solution for you. It might be right for Elizabeth Gilbert, Tony Robbins, Richard Branson, Michael Jordan, Timothée Chalamet, Snoop Dogg, Jessica Alba, Arnold Schwarzenegger, Elvis Presley, Taylor Swift, Jack Welsh, or Warren Buffet.

But that doesn't mean it's right for you.

Sometimes we don't even realize how deeply and automatically we've internalized external frameworks, rules, and opinions. We must approach the messages and stimuli out in the world with a critical eye. We must take a moment to think about whether we've internalized rules for living that aren't our own.

When you can acknowledge these rules, observe them, and then detach from them in order to apply your own intuition to your own situation, you'll find an ease in decision making you've never had before, regardless of the stakes.

This is the essence of discernment.

Build a Bench, Seek Council, and Triangulate

Still, we don't have all the answers.

As such, we do need counsel.

We do need help.

We do need to rely on others.

When an emotionally-charged situation arises with unexpected quickness, we go on red alert. Our amygdalae go into overdrive. This is when we experience the greatest risk of entering a reactive state rather than a reflective and responsive one.

This is when it becomes most difficult to practice discernment.

The antidote is to build your bench.

Although I never thought I'd use a team sports analogy in anything I ever wrote or talked about, it really is too perfect in this case. And it is similar to how dance companies and Broadway shows work. In sports, the best teams know that their ability to weather unexpected turns of fate in a game is to have a strong bench. We often focus on the starters. Those are the stars. There are sometimes entire stretches of a season when second and third string members of the team don't play at all.

But if you're a wise coach, having those players–or understudies if you're in the theater– on hand, nurturing them, and making sure you communicate with them regularly is what will ensure they can step in and save the day when a key player has an injury, your opponent pulls out an unexpected strategy, or you encounter any other kind of unforeseen circumstance.

A strong bench is a hedge against uncertainty.

When you encounter a challenging situation, especially one the likes of which you've never seen before, having a coterie of experts you trust and have already built strong relationships with eliminates much of the psychological noise that impedes discernment. The real trick here is to have a bunch of experts in your corner who have different strengths so you can weigh their feedback and guidance against one another.

So, how do you know you have the right team members on your bench before a chaotic event occurs? You triangulate. You bring in diverse members of an extended bench on small, low-stakes situations. You try out two potential bench members on the same small problem and compare.

It's worth spending five hundred dollars now to save a million dollars in the future.

The last thing you want is to be rushing around to find experts to guide you when the heat is already up. Have your A-players, your trusted advisors, in your corner beforehand and the clarity you'll achieve will let you play whatever hand you're dealt to the highest level possible.

Typically, we make decision-making all about ourselves, whether we know it or not. We obsess over what our bad—or good—decisions say about us as people. We agonize over whether our decisions will get us fired or earn us a bonus. We lay in bed at night wondering what our decisions are doing to our reputation.

All of this is ego-based. And it's what gets us in trouble time and again.

At the heart of discernment is humility.

At the heart of discernment is finally realizing we are not in control.

Once we loosen our grip on the reins of life and make peace with the unpredictability of the cards we are dealt, we can begin to truly trust that our Buddha nature will take care of us.

Wrapping It Up

Think like a poker player, not a chess player.

Marry your reason to your intuition. And embrace that all actions have consequences.

Observe your thoughts, and acknowledge your emotions without judging them, and abandon one-size-fits-all solutions.

Build a bench, seek council, and triangulate.

Humbly trust that your Buddha nature can handle what comes up.

A few guiding questions to help you access your Buddha nature:

1. Where in your life might it serve you to think more like a poker player? Write down how you could do things differently with this new framework.

2. Who are the key members of your bench?

3. Next to each member of your bench, write down their go-to modes and inclinations. This will help you know how to bring in their disparate opinions when you encounter an especially knotty decision.

_____

_____

_____

_____

Chapter 6

LIBERATE YOURSELF FROM FEAR

In 2014 I wrote a musical called *50 Shades of F****d Up*—a playful, sexy parody of the (as I see it) deeply offensive and anti-feminist blockbuster erotic novel *50 Shades of Grey*. My version was a musical theater piece with original music and lyrics composed by my dear friend, the brilliant Andrew David Sotomayor.

I was also the show's director and choreographer. Like any professional show, there was a stage manager. Stage managers handle all the logistics, manage the actor's schedules during rehearsals, and keep things on track once it opens, and the director is no longer officially part of the process. They also work with the tech team on light cues, sounds cues, props, music, and all the rest.

The right stage manager can significantly reduce the overall stress level in what is an inherently high-pressure process, while also creating a well-oiled machine. The real pros free up a cast to simply be creative. The best ones make the experience fun for everyone involved.

Ours did not.

The stage manager we hired was, to put it plainly, not good at his job. He was disorganized. He was inefficient. He worked less hard than anyone else involved. Plus, he intimidated other members of the team.

I noticed some red flags early on, but I told myself a story about how we could make do with him. I told myself it would be harder to find someone new than to deal with the situation at hand.

Even I forget my own philosophy sometimes.

Three days before we opened, we had a tech rehearsal. This is where you run through the show with all the lights, sound cues, and costumes to make sure to perfect the run before opening night.

During this rehearsal, our stage manager decided he wanted the cast to pretend to use props to avoid the trouble of having to preset and present real ones.

In short, he was lazy.

I put my foot down.

I said, "Absolutely not, we are doing a run and we are using the props."

He snapped.

He went off on me in front of the entire cast and crew—screaming, yelling, and cursing me out, using the F word. Engaging in this sort of aggression, especially publicly, in front of colleagues, and in a professional setting, crossed every one of my professional and personal boundaries.

I was flooded with emotion. There was shock. There was embarrassment. There was anger.

All of these feelings were immediately clear to me. What wasn't so clear—at least not at first—was the emotion underpinning all the rest.

Fear.

Fear that I would cry.

Fear that I would lose control.

Fear that I would react in a way that would make a bad situation even worse.

Fear that my cast and crew would lose confidence in me or in the production.

Fear that if I responded strongly, I might get badmouthed throughout the industry.

Fear about what would happen if we had to go live without a stage manager.

Every cell in my body wanted to react to these emotions . . . to this fear.

I wanted to lash out, push against, fly off the handle.

Instead, I got still. (remember Chapter One?)

In a steady voice, I announced to everyone present we would be taking a ten-minute break.

I found a quiet place where I could be alone.

I became aware of my awareness, which we will get to in Chapter Seven.

I assessed who on my bench could give me guidance.

I decided on the show's producer—a deeply engaged member of our team who I consulted with frequently. I called his cell and calmly told him what had happened and asked what solutions we had available to us.

He shared the union rules that we were obligated to stick with the stage manager through the end of the production . . . unless we bought him out of his contract. To do so would require a sizable chunk of money, which was not in the show budget.

What would you have done if you were me?

Here's what I did.

I called the cast back and we continued with our tech. Then I excused myself and started calling everyone I knew who could put me in touch with another stage manager. Once I had someone, and got on a call with her, I knew she was the perfect fit. The next thing I did was tell my producer, "We have a replacement. Let go of him and buy him out."

No drama, no attachment, no suffering.

The show ended up being a big success despite the last-minute crisis, but there had been no guarantee of that when I made my decision. I had fear of the unknown. At the same time, I understood that my sensation of fear was not the same as absolute reality. It was a warning signal. It provided me with information. But I didn't let the fear make the decision for me. I took control of my fear rather than letting my fear take control of me.

As a result, I was able to make a decision that was ultimately right for the show, for its cast and crew, and for me. Most importantly, I made a decision that was in line with my values.

This was not easy.

It never is.

Fear is one of the most powerful forces on the planet.

It is wired into every species up the animal chain from beetles and lizards to the Great Apes.

It is certainly wired into deer.

Deer are animals driven almost entirely by fear. As prey, they are programmed to be incredibly skittish. At the smallest noise, they jerk their heads up. They bolt before they think, and they run before taking the time to consider their next move.

These tendencies serve deer well in the wild. It keeps them safe from wolves and mountain lions. If they happen to run away and burn a bit of energy when they get a false positive, it's no big deal.

Sadly, in our automotive age, this same fear has effectively created a plague for these beautiful creatures.

Now when deer bolt, they often end up in the middle of a highway full of two-ton machines traveling at seventy miles an hour. The wiring that served them so well for so long to help them evade flesh-and-blood predators is no match for these metal monstrosities.

Today, there are 70,000 collisions with deer in New York State alone every year.

The world has become more complex for us as well as for our forest-dwelling cousins—going far beyond those necessitated by pure physical survival. The fear response has remained the same. However, we humans do have one advantage over other members of the animal kingdom. We are creative beings. We have, over the years, come up with a wide variety of tools, technologies, philosophies, and psychologies to help us bypass our internal wiring in a way other creatures cannot. A Buddhist practice is one of them. There are many others.

Of course, it would be detrimental to relinquish fear entirely. Fear keeps us safe. It acts as a warning light on our internal engines, whether riding the subway or navigating a twenty-first century work environment. At the same time, when we allow fear to take charge, to guide us automatically based on ancient unconscious wiring, we often get ourselves in a lot of trouble.

In many ways, all of the chapters leading up to this one have laid the groundwork for giving you what you need to get fear out of the driver's seat of your life. Now it's time to learn how to harness that same fear to your own benefit.

The Currents of Fear

When the business world was abuzz a few years back about the "quiet quitting" epidemic, fear was barely even discussed as an element in the phenomenon. An exception was Korn Ferry Senior Partner in CEO Success and Enterprise Leadership Dr. Maggie Warrell.

In a 2023 issue of *Forbes*, Warrell wrote an article on the subject called "Leaders Who Manage By Fear Make Everyone Less Secure" where she presents a hypothetical scenario in which a CEO of a large industrial company is investigating a steep downturn of market share in one of their high-growth areas. Eventually, he discovers that the regional Vice President placed in charge of the area had become a dictator.

"Instead of empowering his people," Warrell writes, "he punished candor, rewarded compliance, and insisted on signing off on every communication back to HQ. Control was his modus operandi. Fear was his tool."

Here, Warrell rightly focuses on how management by fear causes dysfunction. Team members begin to cover up mistakes. They become rigid and inflexible. They become detached and uninvested in outcomes other than receiving their paychecks.

What is less obvious is the extent to which so many senior executives are driven by their own fears. What lay at the bottom of Warrell's hypothetical Senior VP's approach was his fear that if he didn't control every aspect of the operation, it would all far apart.

It was this fear, above all, that spread through his department like a virus.

"No organization outperforms its leaders," Warrell writes. "Yet far too often, rather than inspiring bold thinking, leaders crush it. They shut down conflict . . . They second-guess subordinates' decisions. They marginalize those who don't fall in line behind them. In the process, they ratchet up fear, drive blind compliance, and dampen the very enthusiasm and ingenuity that's most needed. Engagement goes down, *quiet quitting goes up*."

Fear is always present. Often the leaders who strut and bellow the most are, in fact, the most fearful. Fear can cause people to attack and overreact when a more measured approach is called for. On the other hand, fear can paralyze you, causing you to shrink when action is needed.

When primal fear is activated, we often get tossed about in its currents, banging between the banks of fight on one side and flight on the other (think of Dan Siegel's river from Chapter One). Instead, we need to master every tool at our disposal to calm the currents so we can navigate down the river's middle, where fear might be present but where we are not being flung haphazardly about it.

When you are faced with some of the most daunting challenges of leadership, there's a good chance fear is somehow involved. What follows is a process you can use to help you systematically harness and use fear to your benefit rather than letting it harness and control you.

Step 1: Acknowledge the Physiological Response

How do we *really* know if fear is in charge when a challenging situation arises?

It can be difficult since it manifests in so many ways, but there are a few clues.

Ultimately, fear is physical. When an external circumstance triggers our fear response, our adrenal glands flood every part of our bodies with the hormone cortisol. The role of cortisol is to get you into a state where you can fight or flee.

All of this shows up in very concrete form. The tightness in your chest. The knot in your stomach—or sometimes outright nausea. Twitchiness. Shallow breathing. Shaky hands. Heat.

None of these are pleasant sensations. It is this way by design. Our brain and body want us to do whatever we can to relieve them as quickly as possible, which we usually do through some form of attacking or retreating.

The problem is, in modern life these discomfort-reducing, cortisol-dispelling behaviors are not always—almost never, in fact—the wisest course.

Taking the time to observe these physical symptoms serves two purposes.

One, it is a form of getting still. It is a way of putting a beat between stimulus and response. And two, when you get into the habit of acknowledging that what you are feeling is physical, it diffuses its realness. That which we fear often feels utterly real to us—as real as a wolf on our tails. When we acknowledge that what's happening is actually happening *inside* of us, it lets us know that, at base, the fear is simply a sensation—not an accurate reflection of the threat we might be perceiving—consciously or unconsciously—from the outside world.

Step 2: Pause Before Responding

When a dancer wants to have the ultimate ballon, which is our term for "height", we don't just jump into the air. We first root ourselves into the ground, engage our muscles, and take a plié. This gives us the power we need to get as high as possible.

Placing space between trigger and action will have a similar effect in our roles as leaders. Getting still, practicing detachment, and embodying impermanence do as well.

Or, you can borrow from my theatrical background. That's where I learned the value of "taking five" (or ten).

Learn to call for a "take five" or a "take ten." Make it the rule rather than the exception. It will save you a world of heartache.

Step 3: Have Compassion

Everyone is the hero in their own story. However inappropriate you feel someone's behavior is, they usually have reasons for what they do, if only in their own minds.

Just because you have compassion for these reasons doesn't mean you have to agree with them.

Being led by fear dictates that you see people or situations that have the potential to affect you adversely as your enemies. And what do we do to enemies? We try to eliminate or destroy them. In addition to the fact that a bunch of people going around in destructive mode isn't good for anyone involved (or our communities or the earth as a whole), it isn't wise. Because, it's not always—not usually—what serves your own purposes.

Compassion, on the other hand, goes a few steps further than even empathy. We seek to understand where the reality—the behaviors—we find ourselves surrounded by are coming from. We then work to resolve the situation in a way that creates the most value for the most people.

Now, it is worth noting that compassion is not the same as surrender. Far from it. Seeing a situation in all its dimensions is not the same as abdicating responsibility for its resolution. As you might remember from the story at the beginning of this chapter, I acted decisively. I acted in a way that not everyone was happy with.

Still, compassion let me check in with myself and discover whether I was doing what I had to do for the right reasons—the wise reasons. To add value. To serve what we were creating. Compassion allowed me to act in service of higher goals rather than in service of fight or flight.

Develop your compassion. Deploy it to your own benefit and to the benefit of those around you.

Step 4: Make an Informed Decision

By this point, you have calmed your nervous system, taken back space, observed, and used compassion to get a wide-angle view of your situation. You have also, hopefully, called on your resources (your bench), checked in with your past experience, and marshalled your tools.

Armed with all this, you can now make a decision. Fear played a role in getting you here. It told you there was a problem. It showed you that it was time to move. It taught you what you needed to do next. However, this fear did not drive you. It did not cause you to act without conscious attention. You used it, instead of it using you.

And that is the essence of wise leadership and your Buddha nature.

The Confidence/Competence Loop

Before we move on, it is essential that we talk about the role that confidence plays in liberating yourself from fear.

Often, when people talk about being fear-less, it comes down to a discussion of confidence. In many cases, this centers on advice about how you should act *as-if.* Act *as-if* you already have all the knowledge and ability that you need to solve a problem and you will project a sort of courage, at least to the outside world, that will get people to follow you.

There are fragments of wisdom in this. It is true that your bearing does have a lot to do with whether or not people get behind you. If you come across as frazzled, perpetually indecisive, and wishy-washy, it will be hard for people to buy into your vision. At the same time, if you perpetually strut around claiming to know all about areas you actually know nothing about simply to "display confidence," you're going to end up causing chaos—and sometimes outright disaster—wherever you go.

The antidote: Think of confidence and competence as a positive feedback loop, a concept I was introduced to by David Neagle. You need to develop enough confidence to take the first step—to be able to, when confronted with a new challenge, say to yourself "why not me?" And, there's wisdom in keeping that first step small. It will serve you well to take a small enough step to avoid the whole thing crashing down around you but large enough to either see if you've got the skills yet and grow from there, practice the skills you don't already have, or make mistakes and learn from them.

From here, your ever-growing competence will lead to ever growing confidence, which will cause you to increase the size of your risks and grow your confidence even further.

And so forth and so on.

This process will, through incremental steps and incremental growth, dissipate the fear that comes from overload and liberate you to do your best work and inspire others to follow you down that path.

Remember, fear will never go away entirely. The goal is not to eliminate fear but to understand it, work with it, and keep it out of the driver's seat. If you master fear, you master yourself. And that is the key to becoming a truly great leader. A truly wise leader.

Wrapping It Up:

Since you can't eliminate fear, work to liberate yourself from it

    Navigate the banks of aggression and retreat

    Acknowledge your physiological responses to fear

    Pause before responding and then observe

    Have compassion for the people and situations that push your buttons

    Make an informed decision

    Engage the competence-confidence loop

A few guiding questions to help you access your Buddha nature:

1. What are some areas of your life where you regularly beat yourself up? List them here.

_____

_____

_____

2. For each of these areas, how can you reframe them as self reflection?

_____

_____

_____

3. Where are some areas where you could lead with more compassion?

_____

_____

_____

Chapter 7

BECOME AWARE
OF YOUR AWARENESS

When the movie *The Notebook* came out in 2004, I went crazy for it along with nearly every other woman in America. It was a perfect love story. It was the embodiment of how love conquers all.

Or so I thought.

Starring Ryan Gosling and Rachel McAdams as the romantic leads, *The Notebook* begins with the handsome working-class Noah (Gosling) spotting a beautiful, finely dressed young woman named Allie (McAdams) at a carnival in the 1940s. He becomes immediately obsessed. He asks her out repeatedly, and she refuses repeatedly. This changes when he hangs off the edge of a Ferris wheel cart threatening to drop to his death until she agrees to go on a date with him.

Soon Noah and Allie are involved in a passionate relationship, most of which consists of them yelling at and criticizing one another. Of course, there is a lot of making out as well.

Eventually they do break up—at least for a time. During their hiatus, Allie meets a stable young man named Lon. He's a responsible, understanding war hero. Their conversations are warm and devoid of the screaming matches that characterized her interactions with Noah.

In other words, he's boring.

They get engaged, but a short time before the wedding Noah shows up again. Allie runs to see him behind her fiancée's back. Noah shouts at Allie some more. The heat of their interaction is apparently evidence of their love. She confesses her true feelings to her fiancée who graciously steps aside.

Allie and Noah get married and remain so for the next sixty years, blissful together until the end, where they die at the exact same moment holding hands.

The Notebook is based on a powerful myth cultivated by Hollywood and by much of our culture. It is the idea that our emotions never lie. When our hearts pound and our cheeks flush, we must immediately run toward the source of the feeling regardless of any other facts or evidence.

It's a compelling myth. As someone who has been deeply involved in theater for as long as I can remember, I get the appeal.

It is also extremely dangerous.

The internal sensations we call emotions have all kinds of causes. Sometimes they do precede something beautiful. Other times they portend chaos and dysfunction.

The point is, letting your emotions take complete control of the steering wheel of your life is not wise. This is true when it comes to romantic relationships and a whole lot else. Automatically lashing out when we feel anger. Running from conflict every time we feel a tightening in the chest. Sticking with an incompetent employee for far too long because their kindness gives us a warm feeling inside.

None of this is to say emotions are useless or that we should disregard them. They often provide valuable information. But information is not the same as absolute reality.

We are a society more awash in stories than ever before in human history. Stories are delivered to our televisions, computers, stages, Kindles, and phones around the clock. Most of these stories are designed not to enlighten and edify but to entertain. There is nothing inherently wrong with this. It's when we use these stories as models for how to live our lives that the problems begin.

Is it any wonder so many of us end up with dysfunctional relationships, bad business partnerships, unwanted and intractable conflicts, and disengaged teams?

What is the antidote to this pervasive cultural programming?

It is to become aware of our awareness.

What Does Becoming Aware of Your Awareness Really Mean?

As we discussed earlier, human beings are unique in the animal kingdom in our ability to step outside of our immediate experience in order to observe and reflect on our own thoughts.

This is what it means to be aware of our own awareness.

In 2013, the writer-philosopher Gary Lachman expounded on this ability in his book *The Caretakers of the Cosmos: Living Responsibly in an Unfinished World.*

"One idea that runs throughout this book . . ." Lachman writes, "is that at in an earlier stage in our evolution, human consciousness was much more 'embedded' in nature, as animals are today, and we did not experience then, as we do now, separate outer and inner worlds, but a free flowing movement between the two . . . it is my belief that *nature itself* pushed us out of her warm embrace, as a bird pushes her chicks out of the nest, in order to get them to fly. At some point in our evolutionary past, consciousness became aware of itself."

To Lachman's thinking, all that is meaningful and creative about our species has its roots in our ability to step outside of the automatic flow of our feelings and thoughts and pay deep attention to the workings of *how* we pay attention. Yet, far too few of us avail ourselves of this tremendous gift.

In fact, Buddhist philosophy originally came about to help us observe our automatic thoughts, emotions, and ruminations, because so many of us neglect to do so. When we become aware of our awareness, we step outside of ourselves and view our own consciousness at a distance. In doing so, we get better and better at allowing powerful emotions to rise up without automatically letting them drive our behaviors. When we don't have a practice that allows us to become aware of our awareness, we tend to suffer.

This is incredibly liberating. When you get yourself to the place where you can watch your feelings and thoughts rise up in you and simply sit with them without immediately acting, you become truly powerful.

My Own Voyage to Awareness

Like most people who come to dedicate themselves to a spiritual or philosophical practice, I have had my own struggles with becoming aware of my awareness. In fact, it is precisely because I am so passionate about my goals and my projects—because I have such strong feelings about them—that I have worked so hard on developing this skill.

About ten years ago, I was hired to write and direct a one-woman show for a lovely actress. The show was an opportunity for this woman to not only showcase her skills but also to tell her story of overcoming an abusive relationship and how she did that in service of inspiring the audience. We created a work I was proud of and the actress performed it at the Maiden Lane Theater in Lower Manhattan. It had a successful run and when it was over, we went our separate ways.

About a year later, I found out she was putting on a new show. Excited for my one-time collaborator, I went out for a night at the theater to support her.

While sitting in the audience, I soon discovered the show wasn't new at all. Giant chunks of the dialogue I wrote were dropped verbatim into her "new" script. The choreography was stolen from me. The staging and theatricality were mine as well.

Really, the only thing significantly different from our earlier show was that my name was nowhere to be found in the credits (which also meant I would be receiving no royalties). And the new director, who may or may not have known this was not their work, was being given all the credit.

As I sat there and watched this flagrant theft, white-hot rage boiled up inside me. In the days that followed, I replayed the injustice over and over in my mind. I alternated between self-flagellation and plots of vindication and revenge. My mental landscape would have made the Count of Monte Cristo seem like a hippie.

To compound matters, I took it up with legal counsel and they said it would most likely cost me more than I made on the original production to take her to court.

In short, I suffered. The rage, the obsessive thought loops, the fantasies of retribution—all of this trickled down into every other area of my life.

There is a Buddhist concept known as the *second arrow of suffering*. Experiencing misfortune is like getting shot with one arrow. It is painful. But when you attach to the emotion—when you fail to observe it and simply react to it—it is as if you are shot with a second arrow. That's the arrow that sticks. That's the arrow that causes truly deep suffering.

I consider myself lucky that in the time between the experience I just described and today, I have continually deepened my practice. As a result, I have strengthened my ability to become aware of my awareness. And a few months ago, this skill certainly came in handy.

A great deal of my current work is in The Big Talk Academy—a program I have built over the better part of a decade that trains experts, thinkers, and leaders to have stellar speaking careers and become influential voices. Recently, I came across an online ad campaign where somebody used my exact framing, messaging, and verbiage to sell her own speaker coach services.

This time, however, I let the emotions rise up in me and labeled them.

I am experiencing anger. I am experiencing frustration. I am experiencing resentment.

In doing so, I was able to look at what was happening with detached curiosity. I could ask myself, "What information are these emotions giving me? Are my emotions in proper proportion to the events themselves? Is my view of the situation accurate? What options are available to address this?"

I could feel the part of me—that which I call my Buddha nature—take the wheel back from the most primal, animal part of myself.

As with most life-changing practices, this one takes time to get into your bones and into your cells. It requires consistency and it takes repetition. It's those pliés again!

To get you started, I have included some steps you can follow every time you find yourself experiencing an emotionally charged state to make sure you never get foisted from the driver's seat of your own life.

Create a Silence Chamber

When an incident or episode sparks an emotional reaction, find a space where you can be surrounded by as much silence as possible.

Turn off all your devices. Separate yourself from other people. Protect the sanctity of the bubble around you if even only for a minute.

You'll be surprised by how much you can get away with if you simply do what you need to do rather than worrying about how others will perceive you. Most people will give you the grace to step away for a few moments if you need it, particularly if you do so without fanfare.

When you are in the thick of it—surrounded by the chatter of other people and the buzz of whatever triggered your state—it is incredibly difficult to get the distance you need to become aware of your awareness. Giving yourself the gift of silence will make it easier for you to visualize yourself as standing on the outside observing the processes going on in your mind and in your heart.

Label the Emotions

Next, give names to each of the emotions that rise up.

The words you use in talking to yourself about them make all the difference. Saying "I am angry" or "I am sad" creates complete identification with what are temporary states. Instead "I am experiencing anger (or sadness or whatever) arise". This creates the necessary separation.

It is exactly this process of differentiating *you* from *how you currently* feel that lets you become aware of how the inner workings of your awareness works. And like any other skill, the more you do it, the more natural it will become.

Remember, what fires together wires together.

Crafting a Reflection Response

There are three buckets into which emotions almost always fit.

One bucket is *fear*. Even emotions like anger, when we peel one or two layers back, usually fit into the fear bucket. We are afraid, perhaps, that people will take advantage of us in the future if we don't lash out at them first. Or we are afraid we will be punished if we don't retreat.

Sometimes these fears are based in our present but more often they have roots in childhood wounds and unconscious memories. They are usually not appropriate to the situation at hand but emotionally place us right back to when we were younger and less safe. This is not a strong place to act from, particularly for strategic leadership decisions. Fear means our amygdala is in charge.

Another bucket is ego. Even an emotion like sadness can fit into the ego bucket. Resentment certainly always does. Although sadness and resentment are entirely natural responses to external experiences (and certainly in the same of sadness, have their place in helping us process what we are going through), they are inherently a product of hyper-focusing on ourselves. Our loss. The injustice done to us. The unfairness of what happened to us.

The third and final bucket is wisdom. Sometimes our emotions are telling us something we need to hear. Pointing out true danger and warning us away from it. Showing us a real opportunity and moving us toward it. Helping us spark, solidify, or deepen a relationship with one of our fellow humans.

Figure out which one of these buckets your emotional reaction fits into. It is vital to do this because we always want to be operating from our deepest wisdom. Silence helps us clear away the noise that obscures the true nature of our emotions. Labeling it lets us detach, observe, and gain clarity. When we align with our wisdom, then we can act.

The Three Types of Capital

One of the most beautiful parts of learning to become aware of your awareness is that it will open up vast stores of capital to you that are even more valuable than the financial kind.

These are *trust capital*, *relationship capital*, and *awareness capital*.

There is a trust recession going on right now. Trust in our institutions is plummeting. Trust in each other as individuals is falling as well. The more of us that can build the skills to become aware of our awareness, the more trust capital each of us—and by extension, all of us—will generate.

Think about it this way: When we let our amygdala-based emotions drive the car, we react automatically and carelessly. Many of these reactions cause harm. When we are angry or fearful, we might berate others. When we are resentful, we might sabotage them.

This becomes even more damaging when we are in leadership positions. If those who report to us or look to us for guidance can't trust that our reactions are coming from a place of wisdom, they will probably start to make other plans even while telling us what we want to hear.

Related to trust capital, relationship capital is at the core of all professional success. You cannot lead without having an account of relationship capital. Every time you react automatically and carelessly with your current emotional state in the driver seat, you are in danger of reducing that account. And even if your state is temporary, your reaction leaves scar tissue.

Attention capital is the intentional investment of our focused presence.

At the core of any successful career is the ability to do great focused work. However, when we don't have awareness of our awareness, we perceive all of the various tugs at our attention as concrete, real, and unavoidable, which gets in the way.

Attention is one of the most valuable and limited resources we have—yet we often spend it carelessly. We check our phones during conversations, multitask in meetings, and fail in a thousand different ways to focus on the people in front of us.

When the email alert dings while we're working on an important client project and the tightness rises up in our chests signifying "this could be important," we inevitably run and check it. When an "urgent news alert" beckons to us from social media, and a sensation of danger rises up even though the incident is occurring halfway around the world, our flow is broken.

The problem, particularly for leaders, is that we relinquish our attention to whatever exerts the strongest pull on our internal states rather than what we choose to give our attention to. When we fail to consciously decide to focus our attention on the people, tasks, and responsibilities that are most important, we lose trust and weaken our relationships

When, on the other hand, we reclaim our attention, we increase our capacity to connect, create, and lead with wisdom.

Most of us leak attention capital without realizing it. Devices are designed to hijack our reward systems—producing habitual urges to check, swipe, or scroll. These behaviors feel automatic.

The good news is, each of us possesses the ability to tap into meta-awareness that allows us to pause and say: "Wait. Do I really need to act on this urge? Or can I choose to stay present?"

That moment of conscious recognition—the awareness of awareness—is what makes attention capital possible. Without it, we're reactive. With it, we gain the power to direct our focus intentionally.

Attention capital isn't just about digital distraction. It includes any force—internal or external—that fragments our presence. A meowing cat, an unresolved emotion, a nagging thought about a to-do list—all of these pull at our focus. The key is discernment: becoming conscious of what's pulling at your attention and making proactive decisions about where to place it.

Attention capital is an energetic investment in others. And like any form of capital, it compounds. The more you build it—by putting away your phone, turning off notifications, honoring silence before a meeting—the more you bring a sense of clarity and care into every interaction. You show up, not just physically, but emotionally and spiritually. And that changes everything.

When you feel the pull of distraction, create a silence chamber and label the emotion. The mechanics of the email or news alert and how it was crafted to inflame your emotions will become transparent, which will empower you to resist it.

Take deliberate action. Get behind the wheel of your own time and your own life. Your team, your family, your friends, your customers, your clients will thank you for it.

Wrapping It Up

Recognize that emotions are not the same as reality.

Create a silence chamber. When a difficult situation arises and you experience a powerful internal state, find a way to find silence.

Label your emotions. Instead of letting your internal states tug you into immediate action, give them names.

Pay attention to your language. "I am experiencing anger emerge" is a much wiser way of talking to yourself than "I am angry".

Craft a reflection-response by distinguishing between whether your current internal state comes from a place of fear, ego, or wisdom.

Once you become aware that your emotional state is coming from a place of wisdom, this is an indicator that it might be time to act.

Generate, preserve, and cherish your accounts of trust capital, relationship capital, and attention capital.

A few guiding questions to help you access your Buddha nature:

1. What are some areas where you have built considerable **trust capital**? What are some ways you can expand it using some of the ideas in this chapter?

2. What are some areas where you have built considerable **relationship capital**? What are some ways you can expand it using some of the ideas in this chapter?

3. What are some areas where you have built considerable **attention capital**? What are some ways you can expand it using some of the ideas in this chapter?

Chapter 8
RECOGNIZE ONENESS

Jeff Bezos is one of the smartest leaders around.

Beginning from his earliest days, he has smashed every milestone of achievement. Valedictorian. National Merit Scholar. Winner of the prestigious statewide Silver Knight Award for Science and Technology. Acceptance to Princeton University.

At every stage, he assessed, planned, strategized, and attained.

During his time at Princeton, he decided to abandon his lifelong dream of going into theoretical physics, calculating that a career in finance would give him superior returns. He joined a hedge fund, where he specialized in mathematical modeling and attained the rank of senior vice president with breakneck speed.

After working at the fund for a number of years, Bezos noticed data indicating that internet usage was growing by 2300% per year. Unable to ignore this quantitative reality, Bezos left his finance job in 1994 to found a new online bookstore called Amazon.com.

Why did Jeff Bezos choose books for his initial foray into online commerce? Was it because of a deep and abiding love of literature?

A drive to use a transformative technology to spread sublime expressions of the written word throughout the world?

Of course not.

During a 1997 interview at a Special Libraries Association conference, Bezos explained that in the book category, "there are more items than there are in any other category, by far . . . there are over 3 million different books worldwide active in print at any given time across all languages, [and] more than 1.5 million in English alone."

In other words, focusing on books was the *smart* choice.

We all know what came next.

Amazon grew into one of the world's largest—and most dominant—companies, expanding into nearly every sector. The organization has transformed society, decimating much of the brick-and-mortar retail industry and training us all to expect to receive any product we want within one to three days.

It also turned Bezos into one of the richest people on earth.

According to a report by the National Employment Law Project, "Amazon workers around the country have reported being subject to unsustainably fast productivity requirements resulting in injury and exhaustion. Workers describe pushing their bodies to the brink to avoid automatic termination for missing quotas. Data from the company's own records have confirmed their accounts showing that Amazon warehouses have stunningly high injury rates."

Furthermore, Amazon drivers often report having to urinate in bottles in order to make their grueling delivery quotas.

One military veteran, Ted Johnson, who handled deliveries for the company, explained, "I fought in Iraq and Afghanistan and being deployed was better than [the anxiety of] working for Amazon."

Stringent calculations guide everything at Amazon, regardless of the human cost. Employee behavior is controlled by a rigorous, inflexible point system. Lunch is thirty minutes long and if you arrive back on the job at thirty-one minutes or later, you receive a point. Eight points and you are out of a job. No exceptions. Fifteen-minute breaks are timed to the second regardless of how physically demanding the work is, or how long it takes to get from your work station to the designated break area.

Productivity is ruthlessly monitored around the clock via a series of algorithms and surveillance devices, with production rate goals continually pushed upward. Automated management software tracks employees who drop below any designated metric and generate a series of warning letters that scale up to termination.

As described in the National Employment Law Project report, "For decades, Amazon leadership has cultivated a culture of treating workers as disposable parts in a big machine—pushing their minds and bodies until they are no longer useful."

Jeff Bezos has no greater connection to the people who work at the organization he founded—those who haul crates in its warehouses and drive its trucks—than you or I might to our toasters and carburetors.

Jeff Bezos is certainly smart.

But is he wise?

According to a 2024 article by journalist Mark Judge, "the number of people who quit or are fired each year at Amazon is higher than total employment at the company . . . This is double the turnover rate for similar employers and it costs Amazon an estimated $8 billion every year."

Furthermore, in 2020 Bezos was called to testify in front of the United States Congress. The testimony was prompted by an in-depth article written by Dana Mattioli for *The Wall Street Journal* where she investigated, and exposed for the first time, the full range of Amazon's business practices.

Mattioli eventually expanded this piece into a full-length book called *The Everything War*, and sat down for a *Vanity Fair* interview to promote it. During their conversation, interviewer Jack McCordick asked how Mattioli was able to get such in-depth information, documentation, and sourcing on such a secretive and powerful company.

"The turnover and the burnout is much higher than at most other companies," Mattioli responded. "People tend not to last, because it's very aggressive and it can be bruising. As a result of that, a lot of people have come to me—both people still there and people that have left—to tell me their experiences . . . A lot of the shocking behaviors are because of this company's culture."

When success is built on an entirely transactional series of moves that look at human beings as disposable machine parts, it is only a matter of time before those human beings turn on you.

Jeff Bezos represents an extreme example of a philosophy of achievement that has taken hold throughout much of our society. It is the idea—an idea that many of us as leaders have imbibed—that our success as leaders is a result of *our* decisions, *our* moves, *our* abilities. If we work hard and put the right processes in place, we will succeed, and if we fail to do so, we will fail. It is a reflection of the idea that with enough measurement and control, we can shape the world into exactly what we want it to be.

I would argue that there is a far better, more stable, more enduring alternative to a worldview that pits all against all in isolated silos. I call this worldview the recognition of "oneness" and it is based on an understanding of our intimate and integral ties to one another.

What Is Oneness?

Physicists have long understood the interconnectedness of every-thing in the universe with everything else.

The First Law of Thermodynamics states that when energy leaves a system, it doesn't disappear or go away; it simply turns into a new type of energy. This is why we can move a locomotive by burning coal.

The same is true for matter. When sweat evaporates off our bodies, it doesn't disappear. It becomes water vapor, which eventually condenses into liquid water, which, in turn, rains down upon other people farming crops a few counties over.

Likewise, every single object in the universe exerts gravitational pull on every other object in the universe. For example, your coffee cup exerts a gravitational pull on the planet Jupiter and vice versa.

Biologists understand our interconnectedness as well. For example, we are all wired with mirror neurons that literally fire up when we are in the presence of other people, which cause us to experience sensations and emotions in conjunction with others in our species

Pretty mind-blowing stuff. But what could it possibly have to do with leadership?

As leaders, our long-term success and fulfillment depends on how well we understand the extent to which every one of our actions connects with those of every other person in ways we can barely perceive.

It has been said many times that a butterfly flapping its wings in Brazil can, through a series of accumulated chain reactions, cause a hurricane in Florida. Similarly, all of our decisions cascade through the interconnected network of humanity to generate a chain of ripple effects with unexpected and outsized results.

Leaders who keep these potential ripple effects constantly in mind will perform far more wisely than they would have otherwise.

We truly are all one—all of us part of the same integrated system. And it is only by recognizing this oneness that the best leaders arm themselves not only to create value in the present but also in a way that extends far into the future.

A Case in Point

In the 1990s, Microsoft was more or less synonymous with personal computing. Its Windows platform was installed on nearly every home computer, and its one-time primary competitor Apple was practically forgotten by the broader public. When the online revolution began to take hold in the later part of the decade, Microsoft's Internet Explorer was the near-universal web browser.

No one could have expected the decade-and-a-half slide to come.

When founder Bill Gates stepped down as CEO in the year 2000, he was succeeded by Steve Ballmer. Ballmer was every bit the early-Eighties MBA—a true believer in the principles of individualism. Shortly after taking the helm, the new CEO made it clear that ruthless competition of all against all would be the rule of the day.

He implemented a stack ranking policy where engineers were penalized for falling below their coworkers, regardless of their absolute performance. He constantly trashed competitors in public—most dramatically, stomping on an iPhone in front of a big company presentation. He even made a decision to save money by eliminating free towels for employees who used the company showers while simultaneously reducing stock benefits for new employees.

The result . . .

Microsoft cratered.

The company failed to release any significant new products for years. Apple shocked the world by overtaking them as market leader. The few new products Microsoft did get around to releasing, like the Zune digital music player were seen as so inferior that they became a widespread joke.

Ironically, an approach that relied on attempts to dominate, isolate, and crush resulted in less domination, less money, less prominence, and less success.

Finally, in 2014, a decision was made that Ballmer needed to hand over the reins to someone new. Satya Nadella, a division president, was chosen for the role. I think it's safe to say few onlookers expected a revolutionary transformation at the company.

They were dead wrong.

One of the first things that Nadella did when taking the helm was to buy every Microsoft employee a copy of the book *Nonviolent Communication* by psychologist Marshall B. Rosenberg, which championed a form of partnered collaborative communication. This move demonstrated that the age of "every-man-for-himself" was over at Microsoft.

In a short time, Nadella transformed the culture of Microsoft from the inside out—from the smallest one-on-one interactions to the most sweeping business-wide decisions.

According to executive vice president Jean-Phillipe Courtois, "It doesn't matter if you're an executive or first-line seller—he has exactly the same quality of listening."

What was even more surprising to many onlookers was the way Nadella's collaborative, integrated approach radiated to the world outside Microsoft's walls—most notably demonstrated by his launching a string of partnerships with its greatest rivals.

For example, Nadella created a partnership with Apple, under which new versions of Microsoft apps—including Outlook—were released through the iPad. In stark contrast with his predecessor, Nadella used the opportunity of a 2015 event to publicly show off the new Microsoft-Apple apps . . . on an iPhone.

I am well aware that a great deal of this talk about oneness and the unity of all things can come across as touchy-feely or "woo". This is especially true in an era in which numbers rule, spiritual matters are something to be practiced at home in private, and "facts don't care about your feelings" has become a catchphrase.

It is why crush-and-conquer leaders like Jeff Bezos, Steve Jobs, Elon Musk, and Uber founder Travis Kalanick have cult-like followings among many aspiring startup builders, internet influencers, and assorted masters of the universe.

By the same token, it is often assumed that leaders who take a "kinder, gentler" approach are sacrificing results for squishiness.

So, let's take a look at the numbers.

By the end of Satya Nadella's first year as CEO, the value of Microsoft's stock rose 17%.

By 2024, Microsoft exceeded a $3 trillion valuation, only the second company in history ever to do so.

As for the first company to have achieved that honor, it was Apple, from which Microsoft took the crown, to become the world's most valuable company.

The Practical Mechanics of Recognizing Oneness
If we accept recognizing oneness as a given of powerful leadership, how do we make it happen in our own roles?

For one, we have to abandon the idea that leadership is a series of transactions. Instead, we must train ourselves to see that decisions take place within a broader system of interconnection.

For instance, there are times when any leader will need to fire someone. That said, when undertaking this decision, it is vital to recognize that there will be ripple effects on your entire ecosystem. There will be an effect on morale. There will be an effect on workplace culture. There will be an effect on the decisions other employees—and other leaders—make. And if you have built trust capital with your team, like we discussed in Chapter Seven, you will have less overall suffering during this change.

None of this to say is that you should never let anyone go. Instead, it is that you must develop the ability to see clearly the interconnectedness of all decisions, actions, and people should and must affect *how*, *why*, and *when* you make this decision—and *all* decisions.

This is equally applicable for hiring, giving bonuses, providing feedback, sending out office memos, implementing work-at-home policies, making acquisitions, and so on.

Now, it is important to note that plenty of lip service gets paid to the people-first approach to business leadership. Executives and HR personnel regularly talk about how teams are families, how everyone is in it together, and how all of their employees are part of a larger mission.

If you've ever worked in a corporate environment, you've probably heard it all before. However, much of this rhetoric falls flat, to the extent that mockery of these empty words often takes up much of the conversation during office coffee breaks (or private Slack channels) and happy hours.

When proclamations of solidarity and humanity stand in contrast to realities on the ground, it is far worse than saying nothing at all. Calling your team a family a month before a mass layoff doesn't do you any favors.

It is far more effective to work on yourself before crafting your words. Developing a true understanding of interconnectedness and then operating from that basis will get you to the place where the specific words will take care of themselves. If you don't actually recognize oneness, nothing you can say will convince anyone of anything.

When we understand that every decision we make will ripple through unforeseen circumstances in countless ways, we begin to operate from a place where we are reinforcing the foundations and fundamentals of the organizations and teams we are privileged to lead. This is true wisdom. This is how we achieve greatness and build a legacy. This is how we create something that makes an impact and which is built to last.

What are some potential manifestations of this interconnected, long-term kind of thinking? When we truly understand oneness, we emphasize mentorship, abiding relationships, and interpersonal connection. As Satya Nadella shows us, organizations built on this basis substantially outperform those based on aggression and pure transaction.

And while leaders who emphasize the latter may sometimes perform well on paper for the short term, its foundations will inevitably be weak—the kind of weakness will cause the whole house to fall down around them in the long run.

Recognizing oneness also allows leaders to recognize the energy in any space they enter and to understand how profound an exchange of energy can be. In any kind of organization or team, people look to a leader for emotional cues, whether they consciously know it or not.

Whether a leader is angry or sad or joyful, other team members will pick up on this and it will guide the overall energy, as well as overall outcome ... and performance. This isn't to say you must pretend you're a machine without feelings or mood fluctuations. It is only that by recognizing oneness, you recognize that you must acknowledge the reality of energy exchange and find ways to talk openly about emotional realities rather than ignoring them.

A Word or Two About AI

Right now, if you're involved in the business world at all ... heck, if you're involved in the world at all ... you've been hearing conversations about which areas of life and work Artificial Intelligence is going to be taking over.

Will it steal our jobs? Will it become our bosses?

I have no doubt that AI will transform industries (it already has) and become an ever more powerful tool. It will certainly increase productivity. It will eliminate old jobs and create new ones.

But will it replace us? Will it turn us humans into husks who sit around without purpose?

No, I believe with all my heart that this will not happen.

Why?

Because AI will not, and cannot, have oneness with the rest of us.

Our connectedness relies on the fact that each of us has a Buddha nature. AI can certainly process information more quickly than human beings, but it will never possess true wisdom.

Wisdom stems from lived experience and dedicated presence. Wisdom comes from suffering, which we'll talk more about in Chapter Nine. AI does not suffer.

What wise leaders will do as we progress into the future is to use AI to enhance human decision making but will not attempt to use it to replace human decision making. Because, while AI can mimic human emotions, and can even express simulated compassion, it lacks that ineffable quality that makes us truly human.

An Example of Oneness from My Own Life

I'd like to close this chapter with a brief story from my own life that shows you how far a recognition of oneness can go.

We were about to shoot the final day of the documentary feature film *Big Stages* about my work with speakers and their transformation, when Bella, my beloved fur baby, unexpectedly transitioned to be with her sister Lola, who transitioned only six weeks prior. I was shocked and profoundly bereft. The grief was like a heavy blanket that I would not be able to take off. When I got to the set, I had a decision to make. I could have pretended that nothing had happened. Or I could have spent the entire day telling everyone there about it in detail and expressing my intense emotions throughout the entire shoot.

I ultimately did neither. Undergirded by my recognition of oneness, I tuned into the experience of grief as universal, the knowledge that my team would undoubtedly be able to pick up on my emotions if they went unspoken, and also my knowledge of how, as a leader, they needed me to show up and execute on what we had come together to accomplish.

So, I shared ahead of time by letting my team know what had happened, expressing what I experienced, and also telling them that I didn't want to talk about it for the rest of the shoot that day. I knew we needed to get this shoot done in order to wrap the film.

This approach connected us while also giving me the space needed for me to lead us to a desired outcome.

As the shoot wrapped, it began to pour outside on the streets of New York City. And instead of staying quiet with his idea, the Director of Photography and his assistant said, "Wouldn't it be cool, if we shot you dancing outside in the rain?"

And we did. We shot the last scene of me dancing outside in a downpour. Because I opened up such a profound emotional connection earlier in the day, everyone jumped on board. We had a magical serendipitous experience that made the shoot truly special. The rain, which I deeply believe was the collective tears of Lola, Bella, and me, poured down onto me as I danced.

For that moment, we were most definitely all one.

Wrapping It Up

Being ruthlessly smart will often turn out dramatically unwise in the long run.

Ripple effects are very real: Every decision you make has long-term consequences you can't even begin to fathom.

Acknowledging human connection is a strength rather than a weakness.

Recognizing oneness is at the heart of true wisdom.

Talking about people-first is much different than being people-first.

Approach every interaction with curiosity and concern for the whole and you will build a team that will follow you anywhere.

A few guiding questions to help you access your Buddha nature:

1. What are some ways you can recognize oneness in the various roles you hold in your career and your life?

_____

_____

_____

_____

2. What is a challenging episode in your past . . . or one you know you will have to face . . . where incorporating the recognition of the most painful impacts?

_____

_____

_____

_____

3. What is a particular episode from your life where you felt the joy or transcendence that comes from a feeling of oneness?

_____

_____

_____

_____

Chapter 9

BEFRIEND SUFFERING

With the possible exception of the Dalai Lama, no one was more responsible for popularizing mindfulness in the West than Vietnamese monk Thich Nhat Hahn. His books have become bestsellers the world over and luminaries like Oprah Winfrey and Ariana Huffington sing his praises. His ideas are touted by everyone from medical doctors to Fortune 500 CEOs. His smiling face and gentle voice made him seem like someone who emerged fully formed as an enlightened citizen of the world.

The truth, of course, is far more complex.

Born in Vietnam in 1926, Thich Nhat Hahn grew up in what was then called French Indochina, a land which had been ruled by Europeans since the middle of the nineteenth century. The country's economy under French rule centered around plantations with nearly all proceeds funneled back to the mother country. Other than a few homegrown collaborators, most Vietnamese labored under grueling conditions for poverty-level wages.

By the time Thich Nhat Hahn had taken his vows as a novice monk in the early 1940s, a nationalist fervor had spread throughout Vietnam. Thich Nhat Hahn was not immune from these sentiments. Having spent his entire life watching the humiliation and exploitation of his people, he could not help but get swept away by the tenor of the times.

"He said that there was a time when he was tempted to become a Communist," PhD candidate and Thich Nhat Hanh expert Adrienne Minh-Chau Le explained during a 2024 interview in *Tricycle Magazine*, "because he saw a lot of Buddhists writing about the Vietnamese nation but not offering concrete solutions. The Communist-led forces did."

When the Second World War broke out, the Japanese invaded, conquered Southeast Asia, and subjected Vietnam to its own brand of imperial fascism. Once the Japanese were defeated by the Allied powers, the French returned and tried to reassert control, which resulted in an all-out war with a revolutionary army headed by Communist Ho Chi Minh. When the Vietnamese finally achieved victory over France, the country splintered into North and South, which prompted a civil war and American invasion.

Until the 1960s, Thich Nhat Hahn's life mirrored that of a lot of young people of his generation. Many monks became politically engaged and aligned themselves with one or another faction during this period. Thich Nhat Hahn loved his country and loved his people. He wanted justice and freedom to prevail.

However, he ultimately made a different choice than many of his contemporaries who joined revolutionary military organizations like the Viet Minh.

"Thich Nhat Hanh said his realization of wanting to follow a nonviolent path saved him," Adrienne Minh-Chau Le said. "He didn't see violent revolution as the way out. That made him embrace the Buddhist revival as a path of non-violent revolution."

He publicly proclaimed that he would take no side in the conflict. As a result, the governments of both North and South Vietnam exiled him. He fled to France, where he would live for the next thirty-nine years.

In the Buddhist tradition, suffering is distinct from simple pain. Whereas you might feel pain when you, say, break your leg, suffering exists on an emotional level. It is the psychological equivalent of a blanket weighted with lead that you feel you can never take off.

(I do want to add, I am not equating this kind of suffering with clinical depression and mental health challenges. If you are reading this book and are experiencing any kind of thoughts of self harm, please get professional help.)

Typically, the deepest suffering that I am referring to comes from want. It comes from the state where you deeply desire for your circumstances—for reality itself—to be different than it actually is.

Thich Nhat Hanh had spent his life looking for ways to serve Vietnam and its people. He was expelled from it and ended up in the country that had been the source of much of its oppression. One can only imagine this young monk's desire to get back there. One can only imagine his craving for things to be different than how they actually were.

He may have been a Buddhist monk, but he was also a human being. But by working with his suffering as the raw clay from which to form the next phase of his life, he transformed himself into a truly great leader.

While in exile, Thich Nhat Hahn committed himself to extending his gaze to all the people of the world. It was from this vantage point that he came up with the concept he called "Engaged Buddhism."

As religious studies professor John Powers at Australia's Deakin University explained, Thich Nhat Hanh believed "it's not enough to sit on a cushion and meditate . . . that's become a real cornerstone of a lot of modern Buddhism."

All of his subsequent writing, teaching, and outreach was fueled by the idea that if he could help individuals become even a little bit more mindful, the aggregate effect would be revolutionary. When he calmly encouraged people to find mindfulness in the washing of a dish, it was a revolutionary act.

"If you look at Thich Nhat Hanh's teachings," Adrienne Minh-Chau Le says, "they're about being home wherever you are."

In embracing his own suffering, this one leader created exponentially more positive change than the millions of his fellow countrymen who picked up guns and bombs.

The Particular Suffering of Leaders

Every one of us suffers.

When it comes to people undergoing war, poverty, or illness, the reasons for their suffering make sense to most of us. What is less obvious is the suffering of those who seem to be on top of the world.

The movers and shakers. The captains of industry. The masters of the universe. Inhabitants of the C-suite.

Why does the executive who makes her first million immediately begin to agonize over how she is going to get her second?

What explains the Oscar winner who, after experiencing exaltation for a week or two, plunges into the lowest depths of despair wondering how they will ever follow it up?

Why is it so common for business owners to make the not-quite-funny joke, "I love my work *except* for my clients and employees"?

All along the road to success, leaders tell themselves that once they reach their goals, their suffering will finally end. When their achievement brings even more problems and responsibilities, it can become unbearable.

One of the reasons leaders experience an ever-increasing level of suffering is that the more we have, the more we crave. Moreover, leaders must bear the cravings, dissatisfactions, desires, and insecurities of every other member of their teams as well. When they try to take on this suffering directly—to push it away or ignore it—it often grows even more intense. It flares up, festers, and mutates into more destructive forms.

Let's look at a hypothetical example of how this cycle of suffering might come about.

Suppose you have an employee who continually makes careless mistakes. You've already left the requisite buffer time for learning, and they still haven't improved. You've taken them through a continuing education process, you've given them plenty of helpful advice and guidance, and you've paired them with coaches and mentors who you think can bring them along. Still, nothing changes.

But they are trying hard. And they have a family to support.

Now, depending on your temperament, your suffering in this situation might take one of a number of different forms. If you're a certain type of leader, you might rant and rave about *why* this person can't get down such a simple set of tasks. If only they could, everything would be better.

As a result, you become increasingly short-tempered and aggressive with your employee, sometimes even snapping before a mistake occurs. The rest of your team notices this behavior and begins to view you differently. Morale declines. People become afraid to speak their mind and even your most conscientious employees become skittish.

If you're another type of leader, you might agonize about the conversation you know you should have with this employee. You start working longer hours to double and triple check for your employee's mistakes and to redo the work that isn't getting done properly. But still, you allow the situation to drag on. They are such a nice person. They are trying so hard. They really need the money.

Acceptance is key to the alleviation of suffering.

What if instead of resisting it, you let reality *be?* What if you did everything in your power to accept what you were dealing with . . . including the pain involved?

You have an employee in a slot where they probably don't belong. They have repeatedly demonstrated that despite his best efforts, they are almost certainly not going to change into someone with the necessary aptitude to perform at a suitable level for this particular job. In order to deliver on your obligations to your company, and to the other team members who depend on you, you will need to act.

And when you do, your burden will begin to lift.

If you are the first kind of leader in our scenario, you'll no longer feel compelled to strongarm the employee into delivering a result of which they are not capable. If you are the other kind of leader, you will no longer feel compelled to delay or step in and pick up the slack.

Instead, perhaps you will sit down with the employee and collaborate to find a more suitable role for them within the company.

Or, maybe you will create a new role that takes advantage of the strengths you were too blinded by suffering to see before.

Or if you do need to let them go, maybe you can do so in an open-hearted way that minimizes the impact—giving them extra time to find another job while wrapping up any outstanding projects. Not only is there an inherent humanity in this approach; it has the added benefit of keeping morale high. Other team members will see that you will always treat them fairly without sacrificing performance.

The roadblocks you run into as a leader will be never ending. And, by developing a practice that helps you see the world as it is, you give yourself a superpower that others in your world do not have available to them.

Despite how much we might agonize over the problems of leadership, a quick look inside ourselves can reveal how attached we are to them. Our suffering often becomes akin to an addiction. Of course, there is a considerable difference in degree between corporate conundrums and the Vietnam War, but the way the young Thich Nhat Hahn suffered over his attachment to the ills of his country offers an illuminating model. When we learn to detach from the desires that lie beneath our problems, we become at home with— even embrace—them.

Ultimately, it is through befriending our suffering—the attainment of this wider-angle lens—that we can begin to see our challenges not as mere roadblocks, but as the raw clay from which new and exciting solutions can be built.

In short, the befriending of our suffering is the key to true creativity. True peace, true enlightenment and wise leadership.

Suffering and Creative Leadership

Maya Angelou certainly suffered. She was sexually assaulted by her mother's boyfriend at the age of seven. She spent five years in complete silence as a result. She starved and struggled. She bounced from city to city and was forced into sex work as a means of survival.

Eventually from the raw clay of her trauma and pain, she sculpted a memoir entitled *I Know Why the Caged Bird Sings*, which remains one of the most influential works in modern literature. She used her voice to illuminate the lived realities of Black Americans. She was the first Black woman to speak so openly about the intersection of trauma, racism, and resilience.

Angelou became a renowned poet, professor, speaker, and performer. Her work spanned literature, education, politics, and the arts. Her artistic and social leadership was rooted in a profound willingness to stay present with suffering—not just her own, but the suffering of others.

Maya Angelou stepped fully into her pain and, through storytelling, offered others a bridge toward healing and liberation. In doing so, she not only reclaimed her own voice but inspired countless others to do the same. While she didn't call herself a Buddhist, she exemplified what we would call Buddha nature—always leading with presence, courage, and wisdom.

When President Bill Clinton was inaugurated in 1992, Maya Angelou was who he chose to read her poem "On the Pulse of Morning" in front of the United States Capitol—a far road traveled by the silent girl from St. Louis, Missouri.

The Underpinning of All Leadership Wisdom

Befriending your suffering is at the heart of all wisdom.

Everything else we've been discussing before now serves this one fundamental purpose.

Every other leadership principle exists to help you rise to the task of implementing and serving this one.

Why do we learn to get still? Because it is necessary to curb the reactive parts of our minds to work on releasing our automatic tendency to crave and grasp and wish for that which may not be.

For what reason must we learn to embody gratitude? Because suffering is rooted in the ego nature, and gratitude lets us detach ourselves from that ego, cultivating contentment and peace.

Why must we practice impermanence? Because once we internalize the idea that everything is temporary, the fears and frustrations that feel so overwhelming and important in the moment are no longer in control.

Why do we have to practice letting go? Because loosening our grip on the ephemeral and nonessential lets us flow with the present moment rather than resisting it.

We master discernment so we can distinguish the real and essential from the illusory and unimportant. We liberate ourselves from fear in order to free ourselves of what will happen to our ego nature if we fall down, fail, or decide poorly. Becoming aware of our awareness lets us see that our thoughts are just that, thoughts, not defining us in anyway and learning to recognize oneness puts us in a position to see the truth of our connectedness and how our actions, thoughts and behaviors affect others.

As we practice getting in touch with the wisdom of our Buddha natures, we learn how to befriend our suffering. We suffer less. And as our suffering grows less, our Buddha nature strengthens.

All the while your success as a leader grows immeasurably.

Coming Home Again

The Buddhist monk Thich Nhat Hahn was nearing the end of his life. He had lived in exile for thirty-nine years. During this time, he had founded the Plum Village Monastery in France, dedicated to Engaged Buddhism and to the reduction of suffering throughout the world.

Through his work as a writer, speaker, and teacher, he spread the practice of mindfulness throughout the Western World, indisputably improving the wellbeing of millions of Buddhists and Non-Buddhists alike. He met luminaries, world leaders, and icons, including Martin Luther King, Jr., who said publicly that he should receive the Nobel Peace Prize.

He had lived and worked and formed lasting friendships and made unparalleled accomplishments thousands of miles from where he was born and raised.

And then, in 2005, with the permission of its government, Thich Nhat Hanh returned to Vietnam to finish his days there.

"If you look at Thich Nhat Hanh's teachings, they're about being home wherever you are . . ." explained Adrienne Minh-Chau. "But [Vietnam] was a part of his life that he didn't feel he got to complete because he was exiled. It was that desire to return to the roots that made him want to go back."

In many ways, this final action of his life encapsulates the power of leaders who work to alleviate suffering. Thich Nhat Hanh didn't *need* to live in Vietnam to have meaning. He didn't attach himself to that which only the Vietnamese government could allow. Yet by loosening his grip and by leading from his Buddha nature, he increased the sum total of value in the world to such an extent that the great obstacle of his life finally dissolved before him.

It is telling that today his books are sold in practically every bookstore in Vietnam, the country that once spurned him and drove him out.

Most of us are not monks, nor do we need to be. And, as leaders, all of us are working to make an impact in some way, and it is the sum total of that impact that will drive the overall direction of human society.

Imagine what you'd be capable of if you could befriend your suffering and help alleviate that of those around you.

Imagine what the world would look like if you began to lead from your Buddha nature. In the words of John Lennon, "You may say I'm a dreamer. But I'm not the only one. I hope someday you'll join us. And the world will live as one."

Wrapping It Up

True success is learning to be at home wherever you are.

Leaders often suffer even more than others because they take on all the suffering of those they are responsible for.

Your obstacles are the raw material from which the greatest solutions can be built.

Creativity is another word for the skillful alleviation of suffering.

The alleviation of suffering is at the heart of all wisdom.

A few guiding questions to help you access your Buddha nature:

1. What are a few steps you can take to increasingly accept the inevitability of suffering?

_____

_____

_____

_____

2. What are a few instances in your life where pain and suffering differed? Why does this distinction matter?

_____

_____

_____

_____

3. What are some instances in your past where suffering has led to growth or vital learning?

_____

_____

_____

_____

Chapter 10

MY INTERVIEWS WITH BUDDHAS

In this chapter, I let the Buddhas speak for themselves. All of the people who appear here are incredibly successful leaders who have consciously connected with their Buddha in the cause of furthering their life's work. Each of these interview subjects practice formal Buddhism, although they draw from different traditions. The industries in which they work vary as well. In speaking with them, I was uniformly impressed by how thoroughly they embody the wisdom principles discussed throughout this book. What follows are our unmediated conversations . . . with all of their answers presented *in their own words.*

Kasia Wezowski

Kasia Wezowski owns an international training company, a successful coaching practice, and a film production house. Some of the movies she has produced include *Leap*, *Impact*, and *Big Stages*—the latter being a documentary on the personal and professional explorations of aspiring public speakers (which, I mentioned in Chapter 8). She is a frequent guest on CBS, Fox, and Forbes and presents regularly at Harvard University. She lives in a villa in the south of Spain with her husband (and business partner) Patryk, and their two children.

Tricia:

I'd love for you to start by telling me just a little bit about your background. How did you come to do what you do?

Kasia:

There's a lot of lives that I could say that I lived. I was born in Poland. I completed three master's degrees there. Because I studied psychology and also law, I wanted to know on which level I would like to serve people. Would it be more spiritual, emotional, or maybe I would work more on the level of law and human rights?

What I did when I was twenty-five, as part of finding this answer, was go on a big journey to the East. I went to Siberia. I went to Tibet. I rode one thousand kilometers through Tibet on my bicycle. I went to different monasteries and I talked with many, many monks. I meditated there.

I was invited to some places that normally one is not allowed to go because of the Chinese government. But because I was on bicycle, I was invited by people to live with them and to understand spirituality on a much deeper level. I also went to Nepal, to India and to Sikkim.

After my journey, I realized that the way I would like to serve people would be not entirely on the level of spirituality, but also not entirely on the level of law. It would be somewhere in the middle.

A little bit like the Buddha says: the middle path is the best because it's important to be able to express yourself in a rational way when you talk about spirituality. For example, if I would be talking only about chakras, maybe I wouldn't reach the people that are in business environments. And I wanted to reach those people as well.

So, I really went deep into my services as a trainer and also as a coach. I met my husband Patryk and we moved to Belgium. I didn't speak Dutch, so I said, "Okay, let's do the business in English."

We started training people in the U.S., in London, and in all kinds of other places all around the world. We traveled to Singapore, to Malaysia, to Japan, and to Hawaii. Our specialty was teaching people emotional release techniques and nonverbal communication.

We were still spending our winters in India. One day I was meditating on the beach there and I realized something was missing.

I decided it was time to make a movie.

The idea was that we would invite all these great speakers and coaches and spiritual leaders to be part of this journey to show what they can do . . . .and to share their message.

Starting from that initial concept, we created, I would say, a new style in documentary filmmaking. It's not based on talking heads. It's all based on interaction.

We showed all these great speakers and experts in the action of transforming people. And this became our first movie, *Leap*. And then we had the second and third movie and so on. Now we have seven movies that we've produced.

Tricia:

What an incredible journey! How do you think your immersion in Buddhist ideas affected your ability to lead and succeed in all these different areas?

Kasia:

What was the most important for me was that when I was eighteen, I went to the Vipassana practice. This is a ten-day retreat in silence. And it was the first moment that I could see and experience the fear that I had and begin to get past that fear. It let me see that when I got through this fear, I could finally become truer to myself.

I think that one of the great things that the Buddhists gave me was to be able to work with my emotions, to experience them, to be with them, and to transform them.

There are special places in each monastery in Tibet that are kind of like caves underground. They have skeletons down there and they have paintings of [Hindu and Buddhist deity] Mahakala on the walls. When you go there, they play the drums, special music, so you can really release all those emotions and transform them into love and peace and wisdom.

And I think this was very powerful. When you can meditate on your emotions and on your fears, then you can become who you really want to become. You can become a leader who is truly authentic. Then you can share this with other people.

Tricia:

For people who aren't going to sit in silence for ten days . . . or may not be able to travel widely . . . are there any principles from what you've learned that they can apply right away?

Kasia:

The first thing they should do is to leave their mobile phone in the drawer a couple of times a day and sit with a close friend and have a conversation. Just be in the moment. You can always find a good place to drink a good tea and eat something nice with your closest ones.

And the second thing that would help people to access the stillness in them is to be in nature. Because if we are only in cities with the busy traffic, it's the energy of hurry, hurry, busy, busy all the time. I think it's very important that we find our oasis.

It could be a park or even just a small place tucked away. It doesn't have to be in the mountains or at the seaside. You can just sit under a tree. You don't need to meditate. Just sit and listen to the leaves and to the wind. Maybe there's a bit of sun. Just be there for a moment.

This is how we can ground ourselves.

Also, I would say that the most important thing is to connect to the love that you feel inside. When you feel love, you can share with other people with compassion. And you can connect to this love through other activities or other things that you can do in your life.

It could be through connecting with your child. Children can bring a lot of love. Or . . . actually, recently I bought a horse and

I'm sharing a love connection with that horse. According to the HeartMath Institute, horses have larger hearts ... and because of that, connecting with horses intensifies the love. When you are with a horse, love is overwhelming.

These are just two of many, many different ideas. Your pet, animals in general, nature as a whole ... connecting with any of these helps cultivate this compassionate state of being.

Tricia:

I'm right there with you. Still, couldn't you imagine a certain type of hard-driving leader thinking that this all feels a little, well ... soft? Thinking that leadership is about drive and ambition and directing yourself and others.

Kasia:

Connecting to your inner voice and what you really want to do is how you connect to your own inner confidence.

For example, you need to have a lot of confidence to make a documentary. I do all the decisions, and hesitating too much means you would never be able to finish any movies. To find a way to your own confidence, you can do it through self-acceptance and also authenticity.

If the word "love" is too soft for some people, we can talk about authenticity. We can talk about connecting with who you are. With your message. With the kind of mark you'd like to leave behind you.

We can talk about connecting to your values. If you are true to your values and you know what you want, then you become an authentic leader and a confident one. And then people will be more likely to listen to you because they are inspired. Not because they are afraid, but because they are inspired. It's not about control ... it's about inspiration.

Tricia:

That's wonderful. To shift gears somewhat, what does Buddha nature mean to you, and how does it connect to excellent leadership?

Kasia:

Buddha nature is to be flexible. It is to be open to experience and to be able to consciously react. Not out of fear, but out of wisdom.

You can be smart in the way that you are skillful in your area of expertise and at the same time not have wisdom or maturity. Wisdom is closely connected to maturity . . . developing a mature and conscious way of experiencing the world.

It is also based on experience. It's based on your own suffering, because we all suffer. If we can go through our own suffering and be transformed by it, then we can find our own wisdom. And then we can relate more to other people and create more compassion and understanding.

If a person is only smart, but they lack wisdom, they might make decisions that would create maybe more financial success or some increase in technology, but not help the world to become a better place.

Tricia:

If suffering is what connects you to people, how do you get through that suffering to a place where you don't suffer?

Kasia:

It's probably not possible to just get rid of suffering, because suffering is part of us. It is also a part of our nature that gives us some of our wisdom. So, it's good if we can embrace the suffering and transform it, instead of getting rid of it. It's good for us to learn not to run away from suffering, but to accept it as a part of life.

In Buddhism, we know that people get old, they get sick, and they die. We just cannot close our eyes to this. At the same time, we can find love and compassion and joy. Instead of living in the fear of what might happen, we stay in the moment.

And keep in mind that in the moment there's no suffering, because suffering comes from the past. Or suffering is in the future when we think about something that we worry about. In the present moment, there's no suffering.

Tricia:

To push back gently, what if someone, say, broke your heart two minutes ago? Then you're suffering in the present, right?

Kasia:

It was two minutes ago.

Tricia:

That's the fiercest wisdom, Kasia. So, how has your transformation of suffering helped you become a better leader?

Kasia:

I would say that it gave me more understanding of other people, and also why they react in certain ways . . . why they get sometimes scared or emotional. It's taught me how to inspire people . . . .and how to connect to people, which helps me give them more motivation or inspiration.

Thanks to the experience of my own suffering, I can understand other people. If you're a leader, if you have a company, your employees are not just working for you . . . they are complete human beings. There are a lot of things that are happening in their lives. If you can connect with them and understand them, you can find ways to inspire them to become better people.

John Plummer

John Christian Plummer is a television writer. He was the head writer and showrunner on all three seasons for *Granite Flats*, featuring Christopher Lloyd, Parker Posey, and Cary Elwes. He has worked as a writer and producer for NBC, Fox, Bravo, Comedy Central, TBS, IFC, VH1, MTV, Discovery, and the History Channel. He co-created the animated series *Kung Fu Jimmy Chow* and *The Superficial Friends* and has created multiple hit mystery shows for the Hallmark Channel. *Nazarenes*, his original spy drama set in ancient Rome, is in development for Netflix with Sony TriStar. He lives in New York's Hudson Valley with his wife, Maia Guest, and is the father to sons Charlie Plummer, a professional actor, and James Plummer, who attends Loyola Marymount University School of Film and Television's screenwriting program.

Tricia:

I'd love to start by hearing a little bit about how you built such a fruitful career in what is a notoriously difficult industry.

John:

Well, I started out in theater. I started my own theater company . . . the Actor Shakespeare Company . . . when I was twenty-one years old, right out of college and ran that for seven years. It was up in Albany, New York. It was a nonprofit, and we performed in Atlanta and New York City as well. I started practicing Buddhism a few years after that company dissolved with our organization SGI, which stands for Sokka Gakkai International. Now I'm a writer. I write for television mostly. As part of that, I run my own business, which is called Call the Plummer Incorporated.

Tricia:
Great name. Really fun.

John:
Thank you . . . my actual last name is spelled with two M's and no B, but it's the same job. Dealing with muck and keeping the water flowing.

The lotus is the most beautiful flower, but it can only grow in a muddy pond. It's a metaphor for using all the muck in our lives to create beauty. It's a mindset that I think has served me well in my career. We don't have to run away from our challenges, our obstacles, all the crap. We can use it like fertilizer to enrich our lives.

Anyway, right now I'm the showrunner of a show that hasn't started production yet. We're in the early stages of that. The show is called *Nazarenes*, and it's about the early followers of Jesus, about six months after Jesus of Nazareth was executed by Rome in Jerusalem. It's about his followers and features some historical characters, and also a lot of people that I've had to imagine. It's also a spy show, because early Christianity was an illegal movement. They were hunted and under attack, so they had to use subterfuge. And so did the Romans.

I'm working with a production company, which in this case is Sony, and I'm working with a network, which in this case is Netflix, and I'm working with a team of producers. Some of the producers are from an outside production company called Revelations, which is run by Morgan Freeman and Lori McCreary.

Tricia:

So you have to guide a pretty wide-ranging team of people to work together toward a common goal.

John:

The way I see it, we're all leaders. But I feel that my role . . . along with the lead producer, who's a good friend of mine . . . is to set the tone, and then to make sure that we carry out that tone, which is a tone of mutual respect and dialogue. And these are things I learned through Buddhism.

Tricia:

I'd love to hear how specifically your Buddhist practice has taught you that.

John:

I can start by giving you one very clear example. In the Buddhism I practice, we chant every day. It was in the course of beginning to undertake that practice many years ago that I determined I was going to make writing my main focus.

One of the big breakthroughs of chanting for the first time was realizing I'm so much happier when I'm writing. Before then, I was dabbling in writing. Through the practice of chanting, I realized that this is what I really want to do, and I threw myself into it.

Writing is a very disciplined practice. That practice of chanting every day required discipline of me . . . and still does . . . and that helped me become a very disciplined writer.

Then, as I started to gain some success, I would often get notes from people who were paying me. And at first, my response to those notes was, "What the hell? You're wrong. You're an idiot. These are stupid. You don't understand what I'm doing." My ego took over. If ego takes over, it's the most destructive force to creativity.

Around this same time, I became a leader in my Buddhist community. In that role, I'd have to work with people who would . . . you know . . . give each other notes. "Hey, I don't like the way we did this at that meeting. Can we change it?"

There, I was totally respectful of everybody. "Oh, yes, great idea." We'd always encourage each other. "That's terrific. That's great. And here are a few other thoughts that might make it even better."

I mean, we're not Pollyannaish, but the first thing that we always offer is encouragement and gratitude. It makes everybody feel better and then they're more receptive to listening.

Eventually, I realized I wasn't behaving that way at my work. At my work, I was like this egomaniacal monster who was motivated by anger all the time. And I was like, "This has got to change."

We call Buddhism a practice, and it's a practice because you're practicing for how to be in life. And what I realized was, all my practice was for naught because I wasn't being that way in life. So, I was taking an honest look at my behavior, and I thought, I need to be appreciative for these notes. I need to show gratitude. I need to be encouraging to the note-givers, first and foremost.

After that, I learned to really look at the notes and realize that if there's something bothering them, even if they're not expressing it in the best way, there is a signal in that noise. I began to think of it as my job to find the signal.

And if I'm such a smarty-pants as I think I am, then I surely can find the signal in the noise.

So, my practice has completely changed the way I behave with groups of producers and executives. Now I feel that we're united in our mission, first and foremost.

We may be expressing our dissatisfaction with where we're going, but as long as we remember that we have this shared mission, of making this the best show, we can work wonderfully together.

Tricia:

I love that so much. To shift gears slightly . . . as a leader, how do you think about the concept of Buddha nature? And how does thinking about . . . and getting in touch with . . . your Buddha nature help you as a leader?

John:

First, we have to ask, "What does Buddha mean?"

Buddha is not the last name of Gautama Siddhartha. The word means awakened person or enlightened one. It means you're awake. It means that you see the light. That's really what it means.

That, of course, begs the question of what are you awakened to?

You're awakened to your unlimited potential. You're awakened to your interconnectedness with the universe . . . to the reality that you and the universe are exactly the same. We're all made up of the same material as everything else in the universe.

This has all since been verified by physicists and biologists and chemists, but Buddhism has been articulating this for three thousand years.

Also, you're awakened to all these different onenesses . . . the oneness of person and environment . . . the oneness of mentor and disciple . . . the oneness of good and evil. And you're awakened to what we call the Ten Worlds. These are ten different life states that we can possess at any time . . . from hell, which is depression and despair . . . all the way up to Buddhahood, which is ultimate enlightenment to all these things.

So, Buddha nature is really to be awake and aware to all of these connections. I think this is critical in leadership, because it means you're connected to every other person that works on your project . . . in your company . . . in your organization.

Your ability to recognize the interconnectedness of all things means you should be as close as possible to everybody else. It means you don't create distance between yourself and the people you're leading . . . but that you're right there on the line with them.

Tricia:

What does it mean to be a wise leader?

John:

When I was first practicing Buddhism, I was a young man and I was asked to do a study presentation on some material. We had . . . still have . . . these discussion meetings once a month where everybody comes together and they chant together. Then somebody shares a personal experience of how practicing Buddhism is working in their life right now. And then we study something and have a big discussion about it.

I worked really hard on my presentation. I'm a good student. It matters to me. So, I was very proud of myself and I thought I did such a great job. And quite honestly, there was a part of me that was like, that was the best one we've had all year.

After I finished, this wonderful older gentleman, a jazz musician, came up to me at the end of the meeting. He was like, "Johnny, that was so great. You did a great job. You kicked ass."

And I said, "Thanks, Alan. Thank you so much, man."

And then he pulls me in real close and he says, "But I want you to remember something. The goal ain't knowledge. The goal is wisdom."

It really stuck with me because what he was saying in a very gentle, encouraging way, was I know you're very proud of yourself, but take it down a peg, buddy. Don't let your ego get out of control here. And that really helped me at that time. It helps me all the time. Every day I remember that.

Wisdom is the application of knowledge for the creation of value. It's not about knowledge for its own sake.

Justin von Budjoss

Lama Justin von Bujdoss is an American Buddhist teacher and chaplain. He was ordained in the Karma Kamstang tradition of Tibetan Buddhism by His Eminence Goshir Gyaltsab Rinpoche. From 2016 until 2022, Justin served as the first dedicated Staff Chaplain for the New York City Department of Correction at Rikers Island where he provided spiritual support for more than ten thousand employees. Justin has also worked as a full-time home hospice chaplain and is trained in Clinical Pastoral Education, Buddhist end-of-life practices, and spiritual care. He is the Founder and current Spiritual Director of Yangti Yoga Retreat Center, located in Buckland, Massachusetts.

I have studied personally and extensively with Lama Justin.

Tricia:
I would love for you to start by sharing a little bit of your background and history.

Justin:
I'm a Buddhist practitioner and teacher of Buddhist tradition. I've been practicing very formally for thirty years as of this year. And that counts going back and forth between Asia and here to receive

instruction, spending long periods of time in India, and then coming back.

I started really realizing that there was a little bit of an unconscious split happening where I was assuming that everything that was happening in Asia was better or more meaningful or more profound than here. So, in an effort towards developing a much more integrated life, I started to train as a chaplain in New York City.

I completed four units of Clinical Pastoral Education and began working in a hospital setting. And then I started working as a full-time home hospice chaplain in New York. I eventually opened a Dharma center for one of my teachers in Brooklyn. Then I ended up leaving hospice and became the head chaplain for the New York City Department of Corrections.

I oversaw about thirty-three chaplains that work with people in custody. I became the sole spiritual care provider for a uniformed staff of about ten thousand Department of Corrections uniformed staff. Officers, captains, assistant deputy wardens, deputy wardens, wardens, chiefs, et cetera.

Eventually it included about six thousand non-uniformed staff as well . . . what you might call civilian staff. And I did this straight through the COVID pandemic. During this time, I also became the chaplain for New York City's potter's field, Hart Island, and have blessed well over four thousand bodies of New Yorkers who were buried there.

Since then, I've left New York City to work on setting up a retreat center here in Western Massachusetts, which is where I am now.

Tricia:

Amazing. When I was studying with you, one of the things I loved is how you would always open with, "Welcome back. It's a good day. We're all here."

Through that year, there were people who did not come back, who did pass on. And there was something about that opening that brought us all into such a state of presence . . . .at least speaking for me. That was amazing leadership.

Can you talk about that a little bit?

Justin:

Sure. Thank you. I think that all Buddhist practitioners are training theoretically to become a leader at some point because we make this aspiration to help alleviate the suffering of others. That could be done in our everyday relationships if we have partners or if we have families . . . with kids, or with our elders, or in our communities.

Sometimes . . . just like with people in all kinds of different faith traditions . . . we become very fixated on the heroic model of leadership. We fixate on where we would like to go and what we would like to achieve . . . forgetting at times that it's all built on how we relate to any given particular moment at any time.

In Buddhist language, we might call this being present. Being present is really about being able to feel into what is happening right now, and then holding space for what might be happening to the people that one is meeting with.

So, if it's in a classroom setting, it's all the participants. If it's in a boardroom, it's everybody seated at the table.

Sometimes the nature of the violence on Rikers Island would become really palpable and traumatic for people. So, I would check in around that.

Holding space for oneself and others does a lot of things. It creates trust, which I think is really important. It shows people that they are valued, which people tend to appreciate.

It also models that the accomplishment of goals . . . especially long-term vision goals that an organization or business or practitioner might have ... can only be skillfully accomplished by moving one day at a time.

Tricia:

Let's stay for a moment on holding space, which I would say is based on leading from Buddha nature. What would you say to leaders who might say that this seems "soft"?

Justin:

Yeah. Well, for example, I was on the executive leadership team for the New York City Department of Corrections in my role there, and there was a lot of talk about changing the leadership culture. Because it was a paramilitary organization, this idea of holding space for other people was really frowned upon.

However, there does seem to be a relatively undeniable benefit of this ... that when you're holding space, even in a very kind of cursory way, your team feels like they belong. They feel like they're wanted. They feel like they're appreciated.

There's this idea of top-down leadership that assumes that the CEO or the manager or business owner or president or whomever, knows it all. I would say the most effective leaders of all kinds understand that this doesn't tend to work all that well.

From my vantage point ... when I would hire staff for my team at the DOC [Department of Corrections], I would try to hire people who I knew could make a very valuable contribution that I couldn't do. So, part of my comfort zone as a leader had to be holding space for people and managing people that may be subject matter experts in ways that I wasn't.

Tricia:

It seems that what you're touching on is the difference between relational and transactional leadership.

Justin:

I think very good leadership requires attentiveness to the entirety of a team, and that requires being a little slow . . . slow in the sense of like how we have the slow food movement.

Actually, in the tradition I practice, there's this maxim that goes, "practice slowly, arrive quickly". The kind of thinking behind this is that when somebody thoroughly understands what it is that they're doing, how it relates to them, how they feel about it, and how it empowers them, they're able to actually move much more efficiently in their practice. I think this goes very similarly for the workforce.

If somebody feels that they're respected, heard, appreciated, can make contributions, and those contributions can be heard, that person is going to want to show up more and, frankly, work more.

Tricia:

You've talked about ultimately wanting to help people alleviate their suffering. How did this become such a central focus of your leadership?

Justin:

My teachers helped motivate and inspire me to see my work through this lens. Their teachers helped motivate and inspire them. I try to motivate and inspire others so that those people can then continue and do this as well.

The more we're able to nurture other people to be more compassionate ... more present ... more flexible ... more fluid and dynamic in their responses to things, the more that creates a wave of change.

I think that this speaks to building the confidence in having a relationship to a very long-term and meaningful goal as opposed to just building a name for yourself. To just doing this one thing and then cashing out ... or retiring ... and then forgetting it all.

Tricia:

I'd love to move on to the idea of leadership as a function of liberating oneself from fear or befriending fear.

Justin:

It's funny ... I was just responding to somebody who reached out to me earlier this morning about their meditation practice.

In their meditation practice, they were saying, "Well, maybe I should just give up because it seems like nobody around me can appreciate my good qualities."

We all struggle with this, right? How am I being regarded by my peers? How am I being regarded by my mentors? Do I fit the mold of the lineage of the previous partners in this firm or whatever?

This all comes from fear.

So, especially when we're charting new territory, we do sometimes need to maybe put the blinders on a little bit and not necessarily look so much at what all the other people around us are saying or thinking. Sometimes we just need to be very focused on what we need to do in the moment to move an organization forward, a business forward, a lineage forward, or a spiritual community forward.

Again, humans don't seem to be very good at tapping into the long-term view first. The first place we go is short-term, right? And this includes all the stuff about what everybody around us thinks. Do people respect me? Are they listening to me? Are people going to follow me?

These are very natural thoughts and emotions. But the leader has to be able to be comfortable with moving through that.

At the same time, correcting for this can put you at risk for falling into an overly stoic, disconnected relationship to others . . . a very kind of old school patriarchal, stern approach.

What works best is an integrated approach, which requires us to feel. Feeling is a great strength. It allows us to be able to connect with those who are . . . quote-unquote . . ."under us" . . . and who may be feeling similarly.

And we can say, "I actually feel similar to the way you do, and I have a lot of faith in this, and I have a lot of faith in this team that we can actually pull this together."

It takes confidence to appropriately self-disclose some of these feelings and emotions that as leaders we might like to not publicly admit that we're feeling.

A tenth or eleventh century Indian Buddhist meditation master wrote in one text that our difficult emotions should be regarded by the practitioner as firewood if you were staying in a remote forest. The energy of these things we like to just kind of hide away or ignore actually contain a lot of strength.

Tricia:
This conversation has been so fulfilling and important. I'm so grateful to you. Is there anything else you want to share about Buddha nature that we didn't touch on, Justin?

Justin:

I'll just say this one last thing.

I was reading about a master who was very quick to point out to people that going off into a solitary retreat space to recognize Buddha nature is actually erroneous. Instead, it's by bringing your full self to every single thing you do ... whether it's business or having a family or doing both at the same time or being involved in your community ... that gets you there.

Every single moment, no matter how irritating, banal, boring ... that's the place where incredible work can happen in terms of our own fulfillment of our own contemplative relationship to leadership.

And in this particular case, you could say Buddha nature can be distilled at all times from all the experience that we're having. And that is something that wise leaders are able to recognize ... that we can actually regroup and gain clarity in the midst of chaos.

Anika Simpson

Dr. Anika Simpson is a professor of philosophy and, at the time of this writing, the new Chair of the Department of Philosophy at Howard University. She is also Founding Director of Black Queer Everything, an initiative funded by the Mellon Foundation that invests in the next generation of scholars, activists, and artists working toward Black liberation. A graduate of Spelman College, Dr. Simpson is deeply committed to supporting and advancing racial justice, gender justice and LGBTQ+ equity through advocacy and education. Dr. Simpson is the author of *Single Black Mother: Queer*

Reflections on Marriage and Racial Justice (Oxford University Press, 2025).

We were introduced by Lama Justin von Budjoss.

Tricia:
I'd love for you to start by telling me how you originally found Buddhism.

Anika:
Do you want the long answer?

Tricia:
Yeah, all of it.

Anika:
I didn't grow up in a household with parents that went to church, but around high school I started going to a Baptist church in Cleveland, Ohio, where I grew up. That's where I was kind of introduced to the practice of prayer.

Once I graduated from college, I joined a Bible study, but whenever I was trying to pray, my mind would go to what I was going to have for dinner or that I needed to do my laundry. I needed something to help settle my mind so that I could actually pray, which was the catalyst that introduced me to meditation. And from there, Buddhism.

I would say that I didn't do formal practice until maybe ten years ago. By then, I wasn't going to church and I needed some sort of grounding. It first started by seeing Tina Turner's practice in the movie *What's Love Got to Do With It?* I started with SGI, which is her practice. It was good because there's a lot of Black people that practice within SGI. It's a very diverse space, and I have not found that level of diversity in other lineages.

I appreciated that, but I ultimately wanted something I couldn't find with SGI. That's when I found Lama Rod Owen, through him, Lama Justin.

I ended up practicing here in D.C. There's a tiny, little Sangha run by a couple that Lama J worked with when he came out of his three year retreat. So I went there and then later discovered Bhumi Sparsha, which Lama Justin and Lama Rod had started. That was like a love connection.

Tricia:

That's a wonderful story, Anika. When you think about yourself as a leader, how do you think about connecting with your Buddha nature when making decisions?

Anika:

Staying in a space of impermanence helps me not cling to things so tightly. I think this makes me a little bit more willing to try different things. If I try, and it doesn't work out, it's not as big of a deal to me.

So, I feel a bit more confident in my decision making. I don't have as much trepidation. It's not that I'm acting wildly or not thinking through things, but I don't own them so much. I don't take things as personally.

Also, it helps me always try to think of the greater good. Thinking in terms of Buddha nature helps me take the Anika out of things . . . whether I'm working with my department, working with students, or trying to build a program. It's an understanding that it's bigger than me. It helps me silence the ego a bit.

I'll talk about race here . . . because I do race stuff . . . .it was the summer of the uprisings after George Floyd was killed and emotionally I was roiling. The particular Lama at the sangha where I was at the time could not handle the moment.

I remember one session. It was all the Zoom boxes, and I was the only Black face on there. The world was falling apart, or at least America felt like it was falling apart. And I remember the Lama was like, "Well, we can't say anything because Anika is here."

I just lost it. I didn't say anything, but I lost it internally, because then I started thinking, "I guess Buddhism can't hold this."

But then I discovered Ruth King. I don't know if you know Ruth King. She does rage retreats. She's also a Buddhist . . . a Black Buddhist. She was holding something online related to George Floyd. She held the moment and was able to put what was happening in a Buddhist context.

For example, someone on there said something like, "if they're being violent towards us, I'm going to be violent towards them."

And Ruth was like, "no, you can't let any types of hatred or violence keep your heart from being open. And I want to be able to keep an open heart wherever I go. My voice is going to be loud, and I'm going to protest, but it's not from a place of hate and violence."

That was such a transformative moment. I'm not a crier, but tears were running down my face. Hearing that just completely reoriented me.

So that brings me to what's happening now. Even when horrible things are happening, I always want to have an open heart.

Tricia:

I wonder if you could try to connect the dots a little bit to the idea of befriending suffering? Essentially, we all are going to have suffering, and we want to try to alleviate it in ourselves and others as much as possible. How do you approach that?

Anika:

It comes down to daily practice. Yesterday in a meeting, a certain person was getting on my nerves. I caught myself and said inside myself, "May you have happiness and the causes of happiness. ."

Coming from that place . . . which is a way of saying "may you be free of suffering and the causes of suffering" . . . will really transform you. It reminds me that we're just all one.

Whatever emotion is happening is simply arising right now. It's not identical to the "I" . . . to the ego.

Tricia:

Let's talk about that for a second, the idea of ego nature versus Buddha nature.

Anika:

You know, academia can be very ego based. Where have I published? And what have I published? And where are you speaking?

And then philosophers . . . of which I'm one . . . are notorious for being, sometimes let's just say, mean-spirited. They often want to show you why your argument is wrong, so they're going to come very harshly towards you to then say why they're more brilliant than you are.

I think letting go of the ego helps me not be crushed by not meeting someone's standards or what they consider to be super smart.

Before Buddhism, I took it in a little bit more. I always thought, "Am I good enough? Am I smart enough? Does it even sound like I have a PhD?"

Tricia:

And that's ego nature.

Anika:

That is ego nature, yeah. I don't think I was ever on the egomaniac side. I was more on the questioning myself side. Do I fit here?

I still struggle with it. Even with my book that just came out, it's . . . what are people going to think? How are they going to receive it?

Tricia:

Yeah. That's when all the limiting beliefs happen.

Anika:

Yes.

Tricia:

It's not while you're writing it, it's when people get it into their hands.

Anika:

Yes, yes. So, it's been helpful for me to ground myself in Buddha nature even just with that, within my discipline and with my work.

The other thing is modeling compassion. Getting out of the self by relating to one another in ways that are fruitful and having some loving kindness.

Tricia:

Do you find that you are received well when you're modeling this compassion and this loving kindness and practicing your Buddha nature as a leader? Do people notice?

Anika:

Do people notice? There's one woman that I know noticed. She smiles. She's like, "Okay."

I have another colleague that I talk to a lot who's much more pessimistic, I think, in his thinking.

So he'll kind of be like, "Oh, that's very nice of you," or, "Oh, I don't know if I would say that."

I mean, I think it's like he's trying to figure out who I am and why I'm approaching things in the way that I do.

Tricia:

And as somebody who understands Buddha nature, are you able to let go of that skepticism? Clearly you don't take it personally, and that's part of being a really great leader as well.

Anika:

To me it's all a big puzzle. I feel like I sit down at a table and I've got all these puzzle pieces. And now I'm trying to put them all together. Modeling a different way of leading, to me, is just putting together another puzzle piece

Tricia:

And it sounds like that kind of coming together at the table and fitting the puzzle pieces is also part of you in the active practice of helping to alleviate the suffering of others.

Anika:

Well, yeah, because they are suffering. I can feel the suffering, yes. When I came in August as Chair, I met with every person in my department. I heard pain and hurt from everyone regarding some of what had gone on in the past, and I also heard a huge amount of commitment.

So I'm like, we need to figure out how to work with this pain so that we can all work together towards fulfilling our goals and aspirations for the department. It's working with a lot of pain and upset and old wounds. I do see myself in service of helping them work together in a healthy way, whether or not they're not best friends.

Tricia:

Well, from everything that you have shared with me today, it sounds like you are just naturally leading through your Buddha nature. Is there anything else you'd like to close our conversation with before we wrap up?

Anika:

Just that whether I'm on the cushion or if I'm deep into what's happening at work, I come in with the intention of bringing my Buddhist self in, even though I don't always disclose that explicitly.

I have Vajra Yogini there in my office, a little prayer wheel that you can spin. I keep that, as a kind of touchstone. I do think it's important to keep it in the forefront in my workspace so that as people enter into my workspace, I remain grounded in the Buddha, in the Dharma.

EPILOGUE

When I was thirty-five, I decided I was going to stop dancing professionally.

Dance was all I had ever known. It had been at the core of my life since I was seven years old. And, at the risk of sounding immodest, I was crushing it.

I was on the biggest stages in the world. Paris Opera, Vienna Opera House, Lincoln Center, Brooklyn Academy of Music. I was receiving invitations from the most prominent companies. I was sharing billings with legends.

But professional dance is incredibly hard on the body. It doesn't matter what kind of shape you're in or the precautions you take. The repetitive movements required of classical dance are relentless. You are constantly pushing your bones, muscles, and tendons beyond what they are capable of. I was not injured very often, and I still had surgery on both knees and a foot.

I regularly saw colleagues only a few years older than me limping and shuffling around—bodies wrecked, experiencing constant pain.

I didn't want that to be me.

And I wanted to go out on top.

I also wanted to express my gratitude to the world that had nurtured, sustained, and uplifted me for so long.

As I alluded to earlier in the book, I decided to produce and perform one final dance concert and to give the greatest performance I had ever given. I booked the theater, hired my team—stage manager, lighting designer, costume designer, director (Joe Ricci...I love you, Honey) and an understudy. I hired a yoga teacher to warm me up, so I wouldn't have to think about it. I hyper-regulated my diet so I would know what my body did with what kind of food.

Over the span of my career, most of the choreographers I worked with created solo dance pieces especially for me. So, I asked them if I could perform these pieces in my one woman show entitled *Dining Alone*. In addition to their works, I choreographed two solo pieces for myself. I performed each one back-to-back. It was a ninety-minute marathon of all the dance pieces I loved performing throughout my career.

I spent nine months preparing. Just like giving birth to a baby, I wanted to deliberately birth the completion of my dance career.

The theater was packed. It was covered by *The New York Times*, *Time Out New York* and *The New Yorker*. The people I respected most raved about it.

And then it was done.

I wanted to move onto the next chapter.

First, I dove headlong into choreography. I choreographed the movie *Romance & Cigarettes*, which starred Susan Sarandon, James Gandolfini, and Kate Winslet, directed by John Turturro. From there, I moved into directing, helming several documentary short films and countless plays and musicals.

And at a mutual friend's birthday party, Petra Kolber asked me to direct her TEDx Talk. She was very excited and also understood the seriousness of the platform. She didn't know how to structure it, which pieces of her expertise to focus on, or in what order. She felt completely overwhelmed.

At the time, I had zero contact with the world of professional speaking. But I knew theater and I knew storytelling. I offered to help her with her talk. It occurred to me that if I approached Petra's speech like a one-woman show and directed her like an actor, she would stand out.

The talk we worked on together was a huge success, and just like that, the next major phase of my career began.

The next speaker who approached me was, Kristin Smedley. Her TEDx Talk was life altering for her. She went on to speak in front of the FDA, which helped bring about subsequent funding for rare eye disease. And she has spoken in front of Congress on Capitol Hill. At the time of this writing, Kristen even has a new feature film that is winning awards.

I understood the value I could deliver in this new chapter of my life. I launched The Big Talk Academy, an education platform that helps professionals and thought leaders develop the skills to become influential voices and to share their messages with the masses in order to make the impact and the income they were born to make.

I have since been astounded and humbled by the leaders, visionaries, and great thinkers whose wonderful and vital ideas I have been able to help give form.

One is the genius epidemiologist Dr. John Librett, who created his own cancer treatment while in medical school and now runs a company that conducts pioneering research into the reduction of current cancer treatment diseases.

Another is Kathryn Garcia, who as COVID-19 Food Czar distributed one hundred million free meals to New Yorkers.

Then there is Dr. Andrew Benedek, the founder of Zenon, which is the global leader in advanced membranes for water purification, wastewater treatment and water reuse.

There's also Hertha Lund, a litigation attorney and Equine Gestalt Coach who fights for the water rights of the people in Montana, while also helping people heal from trauma with the horses on the ranch. And there's the remarkable Dr. Dwayne Jenkins, GYN, oncologist and robotics surgeon, who is not only saving lives but also bringing meditation and self-care to the forefront of his work.

It wasn't until undertaking this work that it began to dawn on me what kind of legacy I could leave behind. I loved dancing. I love filmmaking and theater. My philosophical and spiritual practice, elements of which I have described throughout this book, gave me an edge as I pursued success as a leader in these fields.

However, I was not complete.

It took a serendipitous encounter with an unlikely prison chaplain, who you heard from in Chapter Ten, to give me the language for what I hadn't known was missing.

Meeting the Lama

For years, I have had a tradition where I take myself to brunch on Sundays and I either work on plays, my clients' talks, or catch up on reading. It's one of my joys, being able to be present with the work, while also indulging in brunch at the bar of my local restaurant in my beloved New York City.

On one particular morning, I was having an egg white frittata and reading an issue of *Lion's Roar*, a Buddhist magazine. I came across an article about a Lama, or spiritual leader, named Justin von Bujdoss who was then head chaplain at Riker's Island.

I became instantly transfixed by his story.

I immediately knew I wanted to make a documentary about him.

I found him on LinkedIn and learned that he lived in Brooklyn. I reached out and invited him to coffee.

He accepted.

We sat down together at Le Pain Quotidien on 55th and 8th Avenue, and I shared my interest with him. By the end of our conversation, he had agreed to let me film him, his family and his work inside Rikers.

Before shooting, I spent several weeks getting to know his family. I quickly became connected with Justin and then with his wife and kids. Next, we got permission to shoot on Rikers Island, where he would be leading a meditation practice with the corrections officers for the purposes of the documentary. Lama Justin threw himself into the project. He put himself out there to help me obtain access. He agreed to speak at a screening I organized at The Triad Theater in Manhattan.

Lama Justin is a humble person. He is soft spoken. He eschews the spotlight. Yet, in this case, he allowed me into his life and his work so that others could see a concept Lama Justin lives each and every day. He told me about his commitment to the principle of "Right Livelihood." And my life has never been the same since. I entitled the documentary *Right Livelihood: A Journey to Here*.

Right Livelihood

Lama Justin explained to me that every decision he makes in his life is based on whether or not it is contributing to furthering his own "Right Livelihood."

As a decades-long practicing Buddhist, I was certainly already familiar with the general concept. It is one of the foundational principles of the eightfold path, which is the Buddha's prescription for alleviating human suffering.

Right Livelihood is found in the morality arm of the Path along with Right Speech and Right Action. According to the Buddha's teachings, Right Livelihood is a way to earn a living that doesn't harm others or oneself. In defining Right Livelihood, the Buddha named five types of businesses that lay people should not engage in.

These were:

- Dealing in weapons
- Trade of human beings including slavery and sex trafficking
- Meat production and butchery
- Business in intoxicants
- Business in poison

Lama Justin views his time on earth through a prism far more expansive than the above prescriptions of *what not to do*. He approaches Right Livelihood as a call to spend his time engaged in proactively *doing good*.

In becoming the chaplain of Rikers Island, Lama Justin didn't simply step away from doing tasks he knew would harm people. He placed himself in a conspicuously difficult situation for the express purpose of increasing peace of mind.

Rikers is one of the most brutal high-security prisons in the country. The levels of violence, and accompanying around-the-clock stress and anxiety, are crippling. Lama Justin understood that he had a gift for conveying the benefits of meditation and true mindfulness in a way that resonated with the corrections officers who didn't tend to come to it naturally and for helping people achieve spiritual insights that might make their unimaginably difficult work with the incarcerated at least slightly less full of suffering.

As such, he moved toward an inherently uncomfortable and difficult situation in order to deploy his talents in a way that uplifted his corner of the universe.

It was the same reason he so readily agreed to help make my documentary a reality. His "Right Livelihood," as he saw it, included the spreading of these messages as widely as possible.

By working so closely with Justin von Bujdoss, the full wisdom of Right Livelihood resonated in the deepest part of my soul.

The Final Piece of the Puzzle

There is a whole lot of chatter in the business leadership and personal development space about the importance of mindfulness and the increased openness to "Non-Western" methods in the workplace. We see this in features of modern work life such as breaks for mindfulness training during the middle of the workday, meditation apps, and in-office yoga classes.

There is nothing inherently wrong with any of this. At the same time, when we focus on deploying philosophy, wisdom traditions, and spirituality solely as life hacks, we inevitably miss their most profound benefits. Despite whatever level of increased productivity, efficiency, effectiveness, and accomplishment you achieve, it won't be enough.

And as a leader, you will experience a sense of "is this all?"

The antidote is leading with wisdom of your Buddha nature. When your life's work aligns with your ability to get paid for it, this is Right Livelihood. When you match your talents and abilities with a quest to make the world an even slightly better place, you will experience fulfillment the likes of which I cannot fully describe in these pages. And this is wise leadership.

You must experience it for yourself.

Now, please note that I am not saying you have to join a monastery or work at a prison to attain your own Buddha nature. And you certainly do not have to renounce material gain. There are leaders attaining Buddha nature in any field you can think of (with rare exceptions) from manufacturing to finance to entertainment to marketing to coaching to technology.

Buddha nature cannot come about through imitation. There are principles but no recipe. Ultimately, there is only your path. What matters is how fully, consciously, and compassionately you walk it.

What keeps you on your path—and off the ego-driven detours—is your Buddha nature. Your Buddha nature will give you a benchmark for making decisions. The more you practice the principles in this book, the stronger your Buddha nature will grow and the surer of the "rightness" of your leadership decisions you will become.

A strong Buddha nature will give you the courage to say no when something or someone tempts you to veer off your path and to say yes to plunging into potential life-changing activity even when doing so gives you a lump in your throat and a flutter in your belly.

And this, above all, is the essence of wisdom.

Wrapping It Up

Not pursuing Right Livelihood is the missing piece that keeps so many leaders from true wisdom.

Spiritual practices as life hacks will only take you so far.

You don't need to abandon material gain to access Buddha nature.

Pursuing your own path with courage is the essence of wise leadership.

A strengthened Buddha nature will allow you to discern when to say no to temptation and yes to adventure.

ABOUT THE AUTHOR

Tricia Brouk is the Founder of three companies, Brouk Moves, an in-home personal training company that she started in 1993, The Big Talk, a professional development platform for speakers and thought-leaders that she started in 2017, and The Wise Leopard, a life-style brand for women of a certain age, while at the time of writing this book is currently developing a new product that will go to market in 2026. She has coached thousands of speakers including former Lieutenant Colonel Alexander Vindman and New York City mayoral candidate Kathryn Garcia. Her work with speakers is featured on Amazon Prime in the documentary *Big Stages*, and she has worked with actors including Kelly Reilly, Susan Sarandon, Kate Winslet, and James Gandolfini. A lifelong student of Buddhism, she lives in New York City with her husband Joe Ricci and their fur baby Eva Moon. When she's not coaching clients, writing, directing, or starting a new company, she's in a cabana by the ocean with Joe being reminded of how much bigger than us it actually all is.

ACKNOWLEDGEMENTS

This book is dedicated to the leaders of movements, companies, boards, educational institutions, communities and families. You are all leaving a lasting legacy and you all have a Buddha nature. The leaders who have inspired me over the years are many. Starting with my team, I want to thank Janice Pawlitsky - your leadership inside of The Big Talk is unparalleled. Katrina Scarlett, the OG of The Big Talk - you know it all and continue to show up. Angelique Santana, Jennifer DeWitt, Sarah O'Malley, Emma Cullen, Liezel Snyman, Emma Price, Forrest Calhoun, Tandria Black, Brandon Tuss, Jess Walman and Aaron Englert - the contributions you make to The Big Talk and to my life are incomparable.

My long time and dear friend Lisa Wheeler - dancer, fitness engineer and creator- the way you lead your team is inspiring and groundbreaking.

My other long time dear friend Jerry Farnett - diners, students, patients, your leadership has always been wise, whether it's offering the night's specials, inspiring our future leaders or consoling an emotional loss. Thank you for your Buddha nature.

My long time mentor and dear friend Sharon McGuire - my dance teacher and budding speaker- you don't even know the impact of your leadership.

My Mom Gayle Brouk - thank you for allowing for the present to unfold as I lead us.

Andrew Bennett - my brother from another mother, your heart and soul lead always and each human you touch through your leadership is wiser because of your wisdom, thank you.

Michael F. Schein - thank you for your vulnerability during our collaboration and co-creation that is truly leadership.

Ekpedeme "Pamay" M. Bassey - I met you on the subway in New York City and from then on witnessed your wise leadership from stages to boardrooms. Thank you for bringing all of us together.

Marshall Goldsmith, your leadership inside of the MG100 is truly inspiring. Thank you for leading the way with your Buddha nature.

And to every community member and speaker inside of The Big Talk. The way I witness you all accessing the wisdom of your Buddha nature to lead and make the world a better place is what it's all about. And for that I am deeply grateful.

REFERENCES

Abadi, Mark. "The 15-year-old book CEO Satya Nadella handed his execs to start defusing Microsoft's toxic culture explains exactly how the words we use can get people on our side — or turn them against us." *Yahoo!Finance.* November 2, 2018. https://finance.yahoo.com/news/15-old-book-ceo-satya-174712937.html

Agence France-Presse. "Buddhist monk who brought mindfulness to West dies in Vietnam." *France 24.* June 22, 2022. https://www.france24.com/en/live-news/20220122-buddhist-monk-who-brought-mindfulness-to-west-dies-in-vietnam

Bushkin, Henry. *Johnny Carson.* New York: Houghton Mifflin Harcourt, 2013.

Cain, Áine. "A 27-year-old CEO says too many company founders get a key element of leadership all wrong." *Business Insider.* August 22, 2017. https://www.businessinsider.com/bumble-ceo-leadership-employees-2017-7

Caryrou, John. *Bad Blood: Secrets and Lies in a Silicon Valley Startup.* New York: Vintage, 2020.

Duerr, Maia Zenyu. "The Dharma of Right Livelihood." *Upaya Zen Center.* November 26, 2017. https://www.upaya.org/2017/11/dharma-right-livelihood-maia-zenyu-duerr/

Del Rey, Jason. "The Amazonification of the American Workforce." *Vox.* April 21, 2022. https://www.vox.com/the-highlight/22977660/amazon-warehouses-work-injuries-retail-labor

Eichenwald, Kurt. "Microsoft's Lost Decade." *Vanity Fair.* July 24, 2012. https://www.vanityfair.com/news/business/2012/08/microsoft-lost-mojo-steve-ballmer

Complete Guide to the Alexander Technique website: https://alexander-technique.com/constructiverest/

Goodwin, Doris Kearns. T*eam of Rivals: The Political Genius of Abraham Lincoln.* New York: Simon & Schuster. 2006.

Greenhouse, Steven. "Amazon fired him—now he's trying to unionize 5,000 workers in New York." *The Guardian.* June 4, 2021. https://www.theguardian.com/technology/2021/jun/04/amazon-workers-staten-island-christian-smalls

Hebb, Donald O. *The Organization of Behavior: A Neuropsychological Theory.* New York: Wiley, 1949.

Higgins, Tim. *Power Play: Tesla, Elon Musk, and the Bet of the Century.* New York: Doubleday, 2021.

Holiday, Ryan. "Why You Should Pretend Today Is the End." *The New York Observer.* June 27, 2017. https://observer.com/2017/06/why-you-should-pretend-today-is-the-end-memento-mori-stoicism-philosophy/

Horton, Adrian. "Documentary uncovers the difficult battle to unionize at Amazon." *The Guardian.* January 22, 2024. *https://www.theguardian.com/film/2024/jan/22/sundance-film-festival-amazon-documentary*

Isaacson, Walter. *Steve Jobs.* New York: Simon & Schuster, 2011.

Jackson, Sarah; Thompson, Polly; Weinberger, Matt. "Satya Nadella's career rise, from computer science student to turning Microsoft into a $3 trillion titan as CEO." *Business Insider.* August 28, 2024. https://www.businessinsider.com/microsoft-ceo-satya-nadella-career-rise

Judge, Mark. "Bezos Gets It Backwards: He Should Run Amazon Like the Post and the Post Like Amazon." *Chronicles: A Magazine of American Culture.* September 25, 2024. https://chroniclesmagazine.org/web/

bezos-gets-it-backwards-he-should-run-amazon-like-the-post-and-the-post-like-amazon/

Konnikova, Maria. *The Biggest Bluff: How I Learned to Pay Attention, Master Myself, and Win.* New York: Penguin Books, 2021.

Levy, Steven. *In the Plex: How Google Thinks, Works, and Shapes Our Lives.* New York: Simon & Schuster, 2011.

Mattioli, Dana. "The Tactics Elon Musk Uses to Manage His 'Legion' of Babies—and Their Mothers." *The Wall Street Journal.* April 15, 2025. https://www.wsj.com/politics/elon-musk-children-mothers-ashley-st-clair-grimes-dc7ba05c?utm

McCordick, Jack. "Inside the Brutal Business Practices of Amazon—And How It Became 'Too Toxic to Touch'" *Vanity Fair.* April 23. 2024. https://www.vanityfair.com/news/story/inside-amazon-business-practices

Pang, Alex Soojung-Kim. *Rest: Why You Get More Done When You Work Less.* New York: Basic Books, 2018.

Ranallo-Higgins, Frederick M. "Becoming Thay." *Tricycle.* Fall, 2024. https://tricycle.org/magazine/thich-nhat-hanh-vietnam/

Sainto, Michael. "Exploited Amazon workers need a union. When will they get one?" The Guardian. July 8, 2018. https://www.theguardian.com/commentisfree/2018/jul/08/amazon-jeff-bezos-unionize-working-conditions

Satell, Greg. "A Look Back At Why Blockbuster Really Failed And Why It Didn't Have To." *Forbes.* September 5, 2014.

Siegel, Daniel J. *Mindsight: The New Science of Personal Transformation.* New York: Bantam, 2010.

Slash. "Call Me Slash." *Musician Magazine*, Dec. 1990.

Stone, Brad. *The Everything Store: Jeff Bezos and the Age of Amazon.* New York: Back Bay Books, 2014.

Ventatesh, Krishnan. "Why Right Livelihood Isn't Just About Your Day Job." August 13, 2017. https://tricycle.org/article/right-livelihood-isnt-just-day-job/

Vidal, Gore. *Lincoln*. New York: Random House, 1984.

Tung, I., & Berkowitz, D. (2020, March 6). *Amazon's disposable workers: High injury and turnover rates at fulfillment centers in California*. National Employment Law Project. https://www.nelp.org/insights-research/amazons-disposable-workers-high-injury-turnover-rates-fulfillment-centers-california/

Trombetta, Sadie. "We Need to Talk About How Toxic Noah From 'The Notebook' Actually Is." *Bustle*. May 8, 2018. https://www.bustle.com/p/noah-from-the-notebook-is-actually-really-toxic-but-the-movie-made-it-so-much-worse-than-the-book-9033244

Ward, Marguerite. "Why Pepsico CEO Indra Nooyi writes letters to her employees' parents." *CNBC Make It*. February 1, 2017. *https://www.cnbc.com/2017/02/01/why-pepsico-ceo-indra-nooyi-writes-letters-to-her-employees-parents.html*

Warrell, Maggie. "Leaders Who Manage By Fear Make Everyone Less Secure." *Forbes*. February 15, 2023. *https://www.forbes.com/sites/margiewarrell/2023/02/15/leaders-who-manage-by-fear-make-everyone-less-secure/*

Wikipedia contributors. (n.d.). "Chinese Democracy." *Wikipedia*. Retrieved May 27, 2025, from https://en.wikipedia.org/wiki/Chinese_Democracy